God's Gift of FORGIVENESS

Larry Yeagley

TEACH Services, Inc.
P U B L I S H I N G
www.TEACHServices.com • (800) 367-1844

Copyright © 2014 Larry Yeagley
Copyright © 2014 TEACH Services, Inc.
ISBN-13: 978-1-57258-770-0 (Paperback)
ISBN-13: 978-1-57258-772-4 (ePub)
ISBN-13: 978-1-57258-773-1 (Mobi)
Library of Congress Control Number: 2014936746

Unless otherwise noted, Scripture quotations are from the New American Standard Bible, copyright © 1960, 1962, 1963, 1968, 1971, 1972, 1973, 1975, 1977, 1994 by the Lockman Foundation. Used by permission.

Texts credited to Message are from The Message. Copyright © 1993, 1994, 1995, 1996, 2000. Used by permission of NavPress Publishing Group.

Texts credited to NIV are from the Holy Bible, New International Version. Copyright © 1973, 1978, 1984, International Bible Society. Used by permission of Zondervan Bible Publishers.

Bible texts credited to TEV are from the Good News Bible-Old Testament: Copyright © American Bible Society 1976, 1992; New Testament: Copyright © American Bible Society 1966, 1971, 1976, 1992.

Published by

TEACH Services, Inc.
P U B L I S H I N G
www.TEACHServices.com • (800) 367-1844

Table of Contents

Chapter 1

Forgiveness— *What Does It Mean?*

Ms. Schalk, my third- and fourth-grade teacher, asked me to draw seasonal landscapes on the real-slate blackboards on one side of the classroom. She preserved my masterpieces for a week, long enough for classmates and other teachers to affirm me. They considered me the resident artist in the Cornwall, Pennsylvania, elementary school.

Arithmetic was another story. Ms. Schalk sent us to the front blackboard to solve problems. Despite counting on my fingers and major guessing, my blundering was in chalk for all to see. The teacher pointed out my mistakes, but the rationale behind the problem still remained unclear in my mind. Her command to erase and take my seat came as a welcome relief, but sometimes my chalk marks remained faintly visible.

After school the janitor washed the blackboard with a large wet sponge, vanishing all the ghosts of my faulty calculations. The next day I could look at the blackboard without shame.

Wiping the slate clean—that's what God's forgiveness means to me. Eugene H. Peterson used this analogy in his paraphrase of Jeremiah 31:33, 34: "This is the brand-new covenant that I will make with Israel when the time comes.

I will put my law within them—write it on their hearts—!and be their God. And they will be my people.... I'll wipe the slate clean for each of them. I'll forget they ever sinned!" (Message).

Time has replaced the old slate blackboards with whiteboards. I hate using them. The fumes from the felt-tipped pens irritate my eyes and the marks don't erase easily. Sometimes the current writing is difficult to read because of the traces of previous inscriptions. But God is not hampered by poor-quality writing tools. His forgiveness eliminates the shadows of the past so they don't blur the clarity and meaning of the present. He knows that we can't grow and be happy when we continue to drag past failures behind us. The Lord knows it is impossible to look to the future with hope and certainty when the past continues to plague us. For this reason He has provided the gift of forgiveness for every person in the world.

Did you notice that word "gift?" Forgiveness means a gift. We can do nothing to earn or deserve it. It does not depend on achievement or moral standing. Wiping away the past comes straight from God's heart. Forgiveness is what God is. That's His nature. It has been said that both heaven and hell contain only forgiven sinners. The difference rests in the reception or the rejection of the gift.

A young Baptist seminarian was having a difficult time adjusting to her mother's death. After the funeral she had to go through her mother's house and prepare for an estate sale. Being an only child, she had no family support in the difficult task. The real blow came when she walked into a storage room behind the furnace. There she found numerous black plastic bags containing all the gifts she had sent to her mother during the past eight years. The mother had opened none of them.

I often think of that young woman and ask myself how God must feel when His gift of unconditional forgiveness remains untouched.

Once I noticed a woman approaching the service counter at a Dillard's department store. In her arms she carried a bundle of new clothing, Christmas gifts from friends and family. She insisted that all the items had been purchased at Dillard's, but the clerk firmly repeated that no Dillard's store carried the lines of clothing in her pile.

The woman's embarrassed husband could remain quiet no longer.

"June," he yelled, "why can't you accept a gift just once in your life? Why can't you accept a gift of love and be happy? I'm leaving!"

The pile of clothing represented expressions of love, whether or not the woman received and wore them. The same is true of God's forgiveness. An expression of His love, it never changes. The Giver cannot withdraw it. To do so would be contrary to God's nature. Grateful persons who know the nature of their own sin and the price God paid to make forgiveness possible can accept it. Or those insensitive to their need and its cost can spurn it.

Forgiveness means a gift. Any attempt to deserve it on my part dishonors God. Every argument designed to make His forgiveness conditional reveals an ignorance of His unchanging love.

Forgiveness involves light-light that invades the dark corners of guilt and shame. It illuminates all who are aware of being lost, last, least, and little. This light pierces the abyss of meaninglessness and penetrates the densest condition of sinfulness.

I learned to appreciate light while visiting hospice patients for 20 years. Take Madeline, for instance. She was bedfast in a dingy room. Heavy green shades at every window blocked the warm Texas sunlight. In the dimness she recited all her aches and pains. She told me that she doubted her family's love and didn't hold out much hope of God being interested in her.

On the second visit I swept into her room saying, "Oh, what a grand sunny day. Let's open up our hearts and let the sun shine in!" Instantly I threw up the shades and placed my dulcimer across my knees. Then I played and sang, "'Heavenly sunshine, heavenly sunshine, flooding my soul with glory divine; heavenly sunshine, heavenly sunshine, Hallelujah! Jesus is mine.'"

Her daughter heard the music and quickly entered the room with her accordion. All three of us broke into singing and praised God for His love. The light turned a morgue-like place into a temple of joy.

God cannot tolerate darkness. Once darkness covered the face of the earth, but God said, "Let there be light" (Gen. 1:3). The darkness of sin invaded God's perfect world, but immediately the light of forgiveness went into action, persisting and insisting on restoration in spite of rejection and rebellion.

The light of forgiveness became permanent through the life, death, and resurrection of incarnate God. "In Him was life, and the life was the light of men. The light shines in the darkness.... There was the true Light which, coming into the world, enlightens every man" (John 1:4–9).

The light of forgiveness promotes spiritual growth that sets in motion a chain reaction of healing, warmth, and welcome. It is the foundation of God's community, enabling it to demonstrate God's true nature to the world.

I saw this quality of light demonstrated in Luray Caverns in Virginia. My family and I followed the guide to the lowest bowels of the cave. There he asked us to stand quietly while he extinguished every light in the cave. After a few moments of total darkness an emotional heaviness enshrouded me like a cold, wet garment. Finally the guide announced that he was going to turn on a light equivalent to one candle. What a difference! Gradually he restored the warmth of full lighting. He concluded the demonstration by playing a great hymn of assurance on the organ that used stalactites instead of pipes. What a contrast with the forbidding darkness!

Forgiveness means transformation at a great price. Sin threatens to destroy our inbuilt capacity to have close fellowship with God. It has short-circuited our communication with Him and others until it has nearly effaced His image, but, thank God, there is a remedy. Forgiveness accompanied by Holy Spirit power restores and transforms us-and enables us to see how much it cost God.

Alister E. McGrath states: "The cross brings home to us the deep hurt and pain which our sin causes God. In Christ, God makes clear how painful and costly true forgiveness really is. The offer of forgiveness of our sins is both deeply humiliating and deeply satisfying. It is humiliating because it forces us to recognize and acknowledge our sin;

it is satisfying because the very offer of forgiveness implies that God treats us as important to him" (*Understanding Jesus* [Grand Rapids: Zondervan Publishing House, 1987]).

God's heart is set on transforming us because we are important to Him. We may never fully understand our value to Him. Ellen G. White observed: "Forgiveness has a broader meaning than many suppose. When God gives the promise that He 'will abundantly pardon,' He adds, as if the meaning of that promise exceeded all that we could comprehend: 'My thoughts are not your thoughts, neither are your ways my ways, saith the Lord. For as the heavens are higher than the earth, so are my ways higher than your ways, and my thoughts than your thoughts' (Isa. 55:7–9). God's forgiveness is not merely a judicial act by which He sets us free from condemnation. It is not only forgiveness for sin, but reclaiming from sin. It is the outflow of redeeming love that transforms the heart" (*Thoughts from the Mount of Blessing* [Washington, D. C.: Review and Herald Pub. Assn, 1956], p. 114).

Forgiveness represents a new way of life, a work in progress, an exciting journey through the valley of self-emptying to the mountaintop feast of God's grace, and to the lowlands of human suffering and spiritual poverty, where we drop judgmentalism and lift the downtrodden and the discouraged. Such forgiveness invites us to be a cooperative partner in God's redemptive activities. I learned this only after a painful struggle.

When I was young I viewed God as a divine scorekeeper. Every night I confessed my obvious faults, then I spent a long time trying to recollect every tiny infringement of the rules. Three and four times each night I slid out of bed and quickly confessed some perceived sin. Frequently I struggled with the thought that maybe I would remain unforgiven if I missed even one wrongdoing. Often I fell asleep while combing my memory for some unconfessed weakness.

Once I heard about a young girl who went through the same struggle. She asked her pastor about it. "Mary," he replied, "God's forgiveness is already yours. Kneel by your bed each night and tell Jesus you are opening your life to Him. Confess your obvious sins, then thank Him for His gift of forgiveness. Crawl under the covers and tell yourself that you are forgiven, not because you feel like it, but because God faithfully promised to cleanse you from all unrighteousness."

That story brought me peace. When I opened myself to the forgiveness that God had already provided for me and then thanked Him for it every day, my focus turned to others. A fatherly lay pastor invited me to join other youth in singing for the sick, renovating a fire-damaged home for a single mother, and helping neighbors. The joy of sharing with others convinced me that God and I were walking together. That realization delivered me from unhealthy introspection. The joy of sharing forgiveness and other graces with people around me produced a sense of completeness.

L. Gregory Jones summed it up well: "Christian forgiveness is not simply a word of acquittal; nor is it something that merely refers backward. Rather, Christian forgiveness and more specifically, forgiveness—is a way of life, a fidelity to a relationship of friendship, that must be learned and relearned on our journey toward holiness in God's eschatological Kingdom. It is a way of life that requires the ever-deepening and ever-widening sense of what friendship with God and God's creatures entails" (*Embodying Forgiveness* [Grand Rapids: Eerdmans, 1995], pp. 66, 67).

The meaning of forgiveness is as broad as there are people who receive the gift. As you read the next chapters, may you discover new meanings of God's forgiveness.

Chapter 2

FORGIVENESS *of God in the Old Testament*

My family moved to a small plantation near the Pennsylvania-Maryland border when I was 12. Nestled in a woods near a small stream stood a slave cabin with one small room and a loft. The 16-room plantation house had a walk-in basement kitchen in which the slaves prepared meals and then sent them to the dining room on a dumbwaiter.

Three years ago I visited the plantation. Someone had completely restored the cabin. I lingered in and around it, hoping to sense what life as a slave might have been like, but the best of my musings yielded only vague ideas.

Since then I have read six books on slavery in which slaves and children of slaves told their stories. Now I have a deeper understanding of slaves and a greater antipathy for the system of slavery itself.

My attempt to grasp how people of the Old Testament perceived God has had similarities to my study of slavery. I studied helpful books about the life and times of the Old Testament Era. (My latest such book has been Bruce Feiler's *Walking the Bible* [2001]). Shortly after my ordination I spent entire mornings in the musty stacks of the library at Yale Divinity School. Many authors were steeped in higher criticism. I had the impression that twentieth-century scholars claimed to know better how Old Testament people perceived God than those who lived in that era.

I decided to explore what people of the Old Testament had to say, especially since Jesus recommended studying and believing the writings of Moses in order to become acquainted with Him (John 5:39–47).

Moses, the author of the Pentateuch, seemed a good place to begin. In Genesis he gave a brief description of Creation and an even briefer account of the Fall of the first family. He pictured God as the initiator of grace. The Lord came seeking the guilty couple. God quickly outlined the plan of redemption (Gen. 3:15) as He listed the consequences of sin. He introduced the price of redemption in symbol when He sacrificed an animal and made garments to cover the nakedness of Adam and Eve. In mercy He guarded the tree of life to prevent His children from being locked into an eternity of sin and misery.

While it isn't wise to build a theological position on what the Bible does not say, it is interesting that Moses makes no mention of sorrow for sin and confession in Genesis 3. He clearly emphasized God's seeking, providing, and covering. It appears to me that divine grace is an eternal stream not dependent on the actions of the human family.

God took a risk by asking the children of Israel to demonstrate His character and spread the news of redemption to all peoples. Moses was the key human figure in leading Israel from Egyptian slavery as God brought them out of captivity by many manifestations of His grace and power. Then the Lord gave them His law of liberty. Lest they adopt a works-oriented approach to their relationship with Him, God asked Moses to construct a tabernacle and to begin a system of worship that would point to the Messiah and teach total reliance on God's self-sacrificing grace.

Some doubt that the priests and early worshipers knew the meaning of the spiritual symbolism in the sanctuary service because we find no mention of the application until the book of Hebrews. Others would think that such an elaborate worship system must have aroused curiosity about the meaning of the rituals and offerings.

Years of Egyptian slavery must have eroded Israel's understanding of the plan of redemption. From the blood on the doorposts to the inauguration of the sanctuary, it seems logical that God would impart the meaning of the symbols to Moses and the priests, who in turn would teach the people. God is a self-revealing deity who delights to inform His people of His plan for making all things new.

In the late 1950s I listened to a professor of mine describe the journey of a guilty sinner from his tent to the sanctuary or tabernacle. Leading a lamb, he made his way to the tabernacle in the middle of the camp. There he brushed aside the courtyard curtain symbolizing the Savior. A priest, also representing the Savior, met the man at the altar of burnt sacrifice. The sinner tied the lamb to a stake in the ground, then momentarily leaned his whole weight on the lamb as he poured out his confession. The priest next handed him a knife, with which he quickly cut the throat of the lamb. The priest caught the blood in a basin. The sinner stood before the priest with blood dripping from his fingers and asked, "Now what must I do?"

"There is nothing more you can do," the priest quickly replied. "Your sin is forgiven by the shedding of blood." Then the priest turned toward the holy place to minister on the sinner's behalf. The forgiven sinner returned to his tent in peace.

Moses undoubtedly perceived God as a forgiving Lord after beholding such ceremonies year after year, but an even more impressive lesson in God's grace occurred when he went up Sinai to receive replacements for the two-tabled commandments that he had shattered. "The Lord descended in the cloud and stood there with him as he called upon the name of the Lord. Then the Lord passed by in front of him and proclaimed, 'The Lord, the Lord God, compassionate and gracious, slow to anger, and abounding in lovingkindness and truth; who keeps lovingkindness for thousands, who forgives iniquity, transgression and sin; yet He will by no means leave the guilty unpunished; visiting the iniquity of fathers on the children and on the grandchildren to the third and fourth generations.' Moses made haste to bow low toward the earth and worship. He said, 'If now I have found favor in Your sight, O Lord, I pray, let the Lord go along in our midst, even though the people are so obstinate; and pardon our iniquity and our sin, and take us as Your own possession'" (Ex. 34:5–9).

His prayer of intercession on behalf of the Israelites uses the Hebrew word *salah*, which means "forgive." It is the first time the word appears in the Old Testament. Altogether Scripture employs it 46 times with no change of basic meaning. Most occurrences of *salah* occur in the sacrificial laws of Leviticus and Numbers. God is always the subject of the verb.

Moses believed that God is forgiving. Later in a prayer for the people he said, "Pardon, I pray, the iniquity of this people according to the greatness of Your lovingkindness, just as You also hast forgiven this people, from Egypt even until now" (Num. 14:19).

How could he believe anything else after the experience on Mount Sinai? Moses had witnessed a major demonstration of God's forgiving grace in the Exodus. Now he heard the Lord Himself declaring His forgiving nature.

King Solomon is another good example of how people perceived God's forgiving grace in the Old Testament. Standing before the congregation at the dedication of the completed temple, he spread out his hands toward heaven and began his prayer with these words: "O Lord, the God of Israel, there is no God like You in heaven above or on earth beneath, keeping covenant and showing lovingkindness to Your servants who walk before You with all their heart" (1 Kings 8:23). Five times during his prayer he called upon God to forgive the people.

If you read Solomon's prayer in its entirety, you will probably be struck by his sense of history and a keen awareness of God's readiness to forgive a sometimes stubborn nation. His own father had committed a dastardly crime for which God forgave him. I doubt that David could have kept this episode of his life a secret. Solomon knew about God's forgiving attitude toward his father, and in his public prayer he mentions his father, but not his shameful sin.

In his benediction Solomon said: "Blessed be the Lord, who has given rest to His people Israel, according to all that He promised; not one word has failed of all His good promise, which He promised through Moses His servant. May the Lord our God be with us, as He was with our fathers; may He not leave us or forsake us" (verses 56, 57). They sound like the words of a man who believed in the mercy of God throughout history.

A most impressive Feast of Booths took place after the returned exiles had rebuilt the wall of Jerusalem in 52 days. More than 42,000 people gathered to celebrate the symbolic end of their exile. Ezra opened the Book of the Law, the people all leaped to their feet, then bowed low with faces to the ground as they worshiped God. On the twenty-fourth day of that month they spent one fourth of the day confessing their sins and worshiping God. In the midst of their prayer they said: "But You are a God of forgiveness, gracious and compassionate slow to anger, and abounding in lovingkindness" (Neh. 9:17).

Hezekiah restored worship at the Temple. He had it cleansed, and reinstituted the celebration of Passover. He must have understood forgiveness as symbolized in the Passover rituals. The governor prayed for the people, saying, "May the good Lord pardon everyone who prepares his heart to seek God, the Lord God of his fathers" (2 Chron. 30:18, 19). The Lord heard his prayer and healed the people. From time to time Israel slipped into apostasy, but God kept drawing them back to Himself.

My favorite picture of God's forgiveness in the Old Testament is Isaiah's vision of the throne room of heaven. Hear the words of the gospel prophet describing his experience: "I saw the Lord sitting on a throne, lofty and exalted, with the train of His robe filling the temple. Seraphim stood above Him, each having six wings: with two he covered his face, and with two he covered his feet, and with two he flew. And one called out to another and said, 'Holy, Holy, Holy, is the Lord of hosts, the whole earth is full of His glory.' And the foundations of the thresholds trembled at the voice of him who called out, while the temple was filling with smoke. Then I said, 'Woe is me, for I am ruined!

Because I am a man of unclean lips, and I live among a people of un-clean lips; for my eyes have seen the King, the Lord of hosts.' Then one of the seraphim flew to me with a burning coal in his hand, which he had taken from the altar with tongs. He touched my mouth with it and said, 'Behold, this has touched your lips; and your iniquity is taken away and your sin is forgiven'" (Isa. 6:1–7).

Forgiveness was so gratifying to Isaiah that it compelled him to speak of it to others, to go on God's errands. I have often summarized Isaiah's experience as the upward look, the inward look, and the out-ward look. Standing in the presence of the Holy God, Isaiah sensed his own spiritual poverty and received the free gift of forgiveness. He automatically looked beyond himself to others.

Isaiah proclaimed God's forgiveness with boldness. "Ho! Every one who thirsts, come to the waters; and you who have no money come, buy and eat. Come, buy wine and milk without money and with-out cost" (Isa. 55:1). He continued his invitation by declaring: "Seek the Lord while He may be found; call upon Him while He is near. Let the wicked forsake his way and the unrighteous man his thoughts; and let him return to the Lord, and He will have compassion on him, and to our God, for He will abundantly pardon" (verses 6, 7).

Eugene Peterson paraphrased verse 7: "Let them come back to God, who is merciful, come back to our God, who is lavish with for-giveness" (Message).

Micah, the younger contemporary of Isaiah, spoke out against the hypocrisy of religious leaders who tolerated idolatry to main-tain their popularity. He supported the work of reform in the days of Hezekiah. While decrying evil he also held out the promise of forgiveness. "Where is the god who can compare with you-wiping the slate clean of guilt, turning a blind eye, a deaf ear, to the past sins of your purged and precious people? You don't nurse your anger and don't stay angry long, for mercy is your specialty. That's what you love most. And compassion is on its way to us. You'll stamp out our wrongdoing. You'll sink our sins to the bottom of the ocean"

(Micah 7:18, 19, Message).

Verse 18 in the *New American Standard Bible* reads: "He delights in unchanging love." The children of Israel changed loyalties many times, but God's love and loyalty remained the same. Micah perceived that God's forgiveness was His very nature.

Some versions of the Bible have Micah saying that God casts our sins into the depths of the sea. In Micah's day that meant *beyond being retrieved.* In today's highly technological society we take pictures of sunken ships. We even retrieve counterfeit foreign currency printed by Nazi Germany during World War II and deposited in a deep lake or recover artifacts from the Titanic at the bottom of the Atlantic. The term *depths of the sea* may not be as final to modern society, but Micah used the phrase to show that God's forgiveness cannot be taken back.

I am fascinated with the word picture of forgiveness in Zechariah 3:1–5. Joshua, the high priest, stands before the Lord. Satan lurks at his right hand, claiming that Joshua doesn't deserve favor. Poor Joshua is dressed in filthy clothes, but that doesn't convince the Lord that Satan's accusation holds water. The Lord orders the filthy robes to be stripped from Joshua's body, then replaced with festal robes and a clean turban. After God rebukes Satan, He gives Joshua good news. "See, I have taken your iniquity away from you and will clothe you with festal robes" (verse 4).

Perhaps you noticed similarities between Joshua's experience and the prodigal in Jesus' story. The father wrapped a fine robe around his son, apparently over the smelly rags. Both illustrations have God Himself covering the sins.

The exciting part of the story in Zechariah is that Satan was at a loss for words. He had no response. God's declaration of forgiveness was the last word.

No overview of how Old Testament people perceived God's for- giveness is complete without the Psalms. David prayed: "For You, Lord, are good, and ready to forgive, and abundant in lovingkindness to all who call upon You" (Ps. 86:5). Eugene Peterson paraphrased the passage: "Give your servant a happy life; I put myself in your hands! You're well-known as good and forgiving" (Message). Parents told their children about the Exodus and the patience God exercised with their forebears.

Asaph, perhaps a cantor and a lyricist, sang the history of God's guidance of His people in spite of their unfaithfulness. Right in the middle of the psalm he raised his voice joyfully and declared: "But He, being compassionate, forgave their iniquity, and did not destroy them, and often He restrained His anger and did not arouse all His wrath. Thus He remembered that they were but flesh" (Ps. 78:38, 39).

These words remind me of a Jewish cantor who came to a health club where I worked as a masseur. He sat in the dry heat room for 20 minutes and then went to the shower room. There he sang captivating melodies that soared higher and higher with heartfelt emotion. He loved to sing of God's mercy and forgiveness. Even while I massaged his tall body he would hum lovely strains. This experience enables me to picture Asaph singing about God's mercy and forgiveness to a people who were often following their own ways.

Many Christians consider Psalm 51 the classic example of how the Old Testament children of God perceived His forgiveness. David openly described his sinful heart, requested the Lord to wash him whiter than snow, and then asked for restoration to the joy of salvation. It is clear that he not only believed in forgiveness but also in the bestowal of power to live according to God's will.

As David prayed for forgiveness he recognized that it was not a reward for being religious. He said: "For You do not delight in sacrifice, otherwise I would give it; You are not pleased with burnt offering. *The sacrifices of God are a broken spirit*; a broken and a contrite heart, O God, You will not despise" (verses 16, 17). David, much like the imaginary sinner coming to the sanctuary I presented earlier, could do no more than fall on the mercy of God.

But in time the sacrificial service became perverted. The people saw the multiplicity of sacrifices as little more than a way of appeasing

God, but the Lord did not need to be convinced to forgive. Forgiveness was an abundant reservoir just waiting to be tapped by open hearts. David knew this, and this knowledge prompted his statement that "the sacrifices of God are a broken spirit.)) In reading the account of his sin and Nathan's visit, it becomes obvious that David's open heart was solely a product of God's wooing.

As I finish our look at forgiveness in the Old Testament, I am compelled to share this encouraging jewel from the gospel prophet. "For He who has compassion on them will lead them and will guide them to springs of water" (Isa. 49:10). Peterson in his paraphrase says that God leads them to the best springs.

My family and I climbed Mount Monadnock in New Hampshire several times. We still talk about it because of the spring at the base of the mountain. Cold, refreshing water flows rapidly from an underground aquifer and empties into a pool with masonry walls. Before and after the ascent we lay on our stomach, cupped water in our hands, and drank. On the mountaintop we found rainwater filling depressions in the granite rock, but we had no desire to drink that stagnant water. Gladly we waited until we returned to the spring to quench our thirst.

God's people in the Old Testament tried drinking the waters of rebellion and idolatry, but nothing could compare to the forgiving and enabling grace of Creator-God. Isaiah cried: "Ho! Every one who thirsts, come to the waters; and you who have no money come, buy and eat. Come, buy wine and milk without money and without cost. Why do you spend money for what is not bread, and your wages for what does not satisfy? Listen carefully to Me, and eat what is good, and delight yourself in abundance" (Isa. 55:1, 2).

The water of God's grace bubbling up from the aquifer of God's love was the life-giving power for all who looked forward to the cross. It is the life-giving power for all who look back to the cross and forward to the Second Coming. Soon we all will celebrate God's forgiveness around the throne of our Forgiver.

Chapter 3

FORGIVENESS
of God in the New Testament

My parents used seasonal tactics to produce good behavior in me. They told me that if I didn't behave, Santa Claus would fill my Christmas stocking with coal. Repeatedly they hummed the song that says Santa Claus is making a list, checking it twice, to find out who is naughty or nice. But their tactics backfired when they took me to see Santa Claus at the Bon Ton department store.

Santa was a plump, jolly man who smiled and laughed. He asked me what I wanted for Christmas, then patiently listened to my long list. Then he concluded the visit by whistling loudly. At the sound of his whistle a little monkey came out of a little house. The monkey was dressed in a cute outfit, including a red Christmas hat. Santa said, "Jojo, give this good little boy a present." The creature entered the little house and reappeared with a colorful package that he handed to me. I slipped off Santa's lap and, believe it or not, nobody took pictures for my mom to buy.

As I left the Bon Ton I asked myself how such a nice man could put coal in my stocking. My visit with Santa took my fears away. I had no more dread of coal and a list checked twice.

Despite the many evidences of God's forgiving grace, the religious leaders of Jesus' day still sent fear into the hearts of worshipers. They pictured God as a list maker and a coal dispenser. Stack up a mountain of good works, they advised, and you'll make it to God's kingdom. Fail, and you don't have a chance.

Their checklist theology backfired when litter bearers carried a paralyzed man to see Jesus, God incarnate. Jesus took one look at the sick man and said, "Take courage, son; your sins are forgiven" (Matt. 9:2).

Some of the scribes muttered to themselves about Jesus being a blasphemer, but He read their thoughts. "'Why are you thinking evil in your hearts? Which is easier, to say, "Your sins are forgiven," or to say, "Get up, and walk"? But so that you may know that the Son of Man has authority on earth to forgive sins'—then He said to the paralytic—'Get up, pick up your bed and go home.' And he got up and went home" (verses 4–7).

The incident awed the crowd. Word of this Forgiver quickly spread, bringing scores of people looking for Jesus. The religious leaders angrily sought ways to kill Him, but Jesus continued to reveal His Father's forgiving nature.

The clergy had turned religion into a lucrative business. Their scheme was to paint a picture of a severe God who must be appeased by many sacrifices. It enabled them to sell the excess meat to local butchers and hundreds of hides to tanners. The sale of animals took place with Temple currency based on a dishonest exchange rate. This newcomer who forgave sins and healed diseases threatened their comfortable lifestyle.

Also, they caught Jesus eating with tax gatherers and sinners. The religious leaders regarded such individuals as beyond the possibility of redemption. Jesus heard their protests and said, "It is not those who are healthy who need a physician, but those who are sick. But go and learn what this means, 'I desire compassion, and not sacrifice,' for I did not come to call the righteous, but sinners" (verses 12, 13). From then until His death on the cross, Jesus publicly forgave sinners and rebuked the leaders who were perpetuating Satan's claim that God is a list maker and a cruel taskmaster. He let it be known that He had no intention of patching up the stiff wineskins of righteousness by works, but intended to present the free grace of God in the fresh wineskins of God's kingdom of love.

At least five times Jesus risked early death by healing and forgiving on the Sabbath. He used the Sabbath as a time to lift humanity's heavy load of sin and sickness. What the Sabbath did for poor sinners was far more important than what people did on the Sabbath. Jesus knew that the people He healed on Sabbath spent the rest of the day praising God and telling family and friends what He had done for them.

Imagine yourself with Jesus when He met a woman being condemned by the very men who had abused her. They clutched stones, ready to carry out the letter of their law. Hear the irony in Jesus' voice as He invites the man without sin to cast the first stone at the woman huddled in the dust. His handwriting in the roadside dirt has a stone-dropping effect. The cowardly hypocrites slink away quietly, until only Jesus and the woman remain. See Jesus drop to His knees beside her, placing His large hands on her shoulders as He asks, "Where are your accusers?" See her shake her head as Jesus says, "You are a child of God. I don't condemn My Father's children. I forgive. Go, my friend, and sin no more."

Your tears flow and in your heart is an unrelenting urge to know the Forgiver.

Blind people received no sympathy from the clergy of Jesus' day. Their religion of righteousness by works had turned their hearts to stone. They had the audacity to chalk up blindness to personal or parental sin. Jesus quickly shot down that idea-in fact, He saw it as an opportunity to heal and forgive.

My favorite biblical story is blind Bartimaeus's encounter with Jesus. I picture him without a friend, climbing a hill overlooking a roadway where Jesus is likely to travel. Most of the hot day he sits, waiting. The sounds of a crowd become louder and closer. People eager to see Jesus crowd the hill. Bartimaeus shouts, "Son of David! Son of

David! Have mercy on me! Have mercy!" Again and again, louder and louder grow his calls. People near him snap, "Shut up, you fool! Jesus won't give the time of day to a sinner like you!"

A hush falls over the crowd when Jesus stops and calls Bartimaeus by name. The blind man is so excited that he stumbles down the bank and staggers to the feet of Jesus. He pours out his history of living in a dark world, but Jesus interrupts his long story by asking, "Bartimaeus, what would you like Me to do for you?"

"Oh, Master, thank You for asking. Of course, I want to see. I really want to see."

Instantly Jesus' strong carpenter hands touch his eyes. Light flashes before his retinas. His surroundings come into focus. Before his newly healed eyes stands the Forgiver, his healer. He jumps to his feet and hugs Jesus. Tears running down his dusty cheeks drop onto Jesus' simple clothes. The tears of humanity mingle with those of divinity. Bartimaeus releases his tight embrace and looks into the face of Jesus, exclaiming, "Oh, thank You! Thank You! I will follow You and tell everyone I can about what You did for me."

My son has written dramas for Seventh-day Adventist summer camps for many years. One year the drama cast acted out the story of Bartimaeus. The week of blind camp was the high point. Just as Jesus called for Bartimaeus to come forward for healing, one of the blind campers yelled, "Go for it, Bart! Go for it, Bart!" Other blind campers joined in the cheers because they had all put themselves in the beggar's shoes.

Can you imagine what Bartimaeus's family did when he came home without his white cane? Have you ever thought about the troubled jabbering among the clergy when the supposed evidence of his sin disappeared?

No one can ever doubt that Jesus gave him the TLC of forgiveness and healing. He took *time* from His travels to *listen*, after which He *cared* and *cured*. Henri J. M. Nouwen said that to cure without first caring enough to stop and listen would have been demeaning to Bartimaeus.

Jesus supplied forgiveness for all of His children from eternity, yet He is able to individualize the reception of forgiveness and healing.

The population of untouchable lepers dropped drastically as Jesus expanded His travels. The priests had to examine every leper who claimed to be healed. They had never seen so many healed lepers come to the Temple before. Of course, healed lepers are not tight-lipped about their experience. The priests received an earful of evidence that the Forgiver was alive and well. The clergy knew that their influence was eroding and that the people were pushing Jesus to become king.

The declaration of John the Baptist—"Behold, the Lamb of God who takes away the sin of the world!"—was surely coming to pass (John 1:29). The people believed it, but the religious leaders became more determined to kill the One who healed sinful lepers.

The apostle Peter's understanding of God's forgiveness really took shape when he warmed his hands with the mocking crowd at Jesus' trial. His sorrowful countenance and his Galilean accent led some to identify him as Jesus' follower. Peter emphatically denied it. As he spit out his final words of denial to the accompaniment of the rooster's shrill call, his eyes met those of Jesus. "The sight of that pale, suffering face, those quivering lips, that look of compassion and forgiveness, pierced his heart like an arrow" (Ellen G. White, *The Desire of Ages* [Mountain View, Calif.: Pacific Press Pub. Assn., 1898], p. 713).

Tears of remorse flowing, Peter raced away and never stopped until he fell on the spot where Jesus had recently agonized with His Father: There in Gethsemane Peter cried out his confession. He must have experienced God's forgiveness to be able to write about forgiveness so well.

"He Himself bore our sins in His body on the cross, so that we might die to sin and live to righteousness; for by His wounds you were healed" (1 Peter 2:24).

"For Christ also died for sins once for all" (1 Peter 3:18). "The Lord is not slow about His promises, as some count slowness, but is patient toward you, not wishing for any to perish but for all to come to repentance"

(2 Peter 3:9). The apostle could speak with conviction about God's patience and forgiveness because he was the recipient of both.

The apostle John was a diamond in the rough when he met Jesus. His boisterous ways masked the potential that ultimately became channeled into a dynamic prophetic role. He would bless the church of his day and the community of forgiveness until Christ returned. Knowing God's forgiveness personally, John wrote: "If we walk in the Light as He Himself is in the Light, we have fellowship with one another, and the blood of Jesus His Son cleanses us from all sin.… If we confess our sins, He is faithful and righteous to forgive us our sins and to cleanse us from all unrighteousness" (1 John 1:7–9).

"If anyone sins, we have an Advocate with the Father, Jesus Christ the righteous; and He Himself is the propitiation for our sin.… also for those of the whole world" (1 John 2:1, 2).

"I am writing to you, little children, because your sins have been forgiven you for His name's sake" (verse 12).

"He appeared in order to take away sins" (1 John 3:5). Neither Jesus nor the writers of the New Testament changed the portrait of the Forgiver previously presented in the Old Testament. In fact, Jesus' living demonstration and the way it benefited His followers actually enhanced that depiction. Jesus' portrayal of the Father's forgiveness reached its peak when He prayed on the cross, "Father, forgive them; for they do not know what they are doing" (Luke 23:34).

I enjoy watching a watercolorist on educational TV. He skillfully mixes the colors, throws down a wash on the paper, then adds various color values to suggest dimension and depth. His final act is to place a frame on the picture. Not just any frame. He chooses one that accentuates the dominant colors in the picture. I always say to myself, "Now, that's a complete picture." That's what Jesus did. He painted forgiveness as He mingled with people of many origins, but He framed His portrayal with the cross. That made the picture of God's forgiveness complete.

Chapter 4

FORGIVENESS—
A Gift of God's Grace

Fencerows were a characteristic of small farms in Pennsylvania before the days of the monstrous machines now used by corporate farmers. They provided homes for birds and small animals. Also they shaded a weary farmer and his team of horses when he needed a break from his toil. The wild blackberries and raspberries that grew among them were the delight of the farmer's wife. The cherry trees were no doubt the favorite part of fencerows for my sisters and me. We had no idea how they happened to be there. Large trees, some bore sour cherries, some light sweets, and some dark sweets. The best tree of all was a dark cherry tree with the lower branches high off the ground. We leaned a long fence railing against the lowest branch and carefully balanced our way onto the branch-all of us except my little sister Rosie. She was afraid to negotiate the fence railing, so she sat on the ground next to her empty pail and cried.

My older sister Lucille told Rosie to stop crying because she would help her. She found a spot where the cherries were thick, filled her pail quickly, then made her way to the little girl's side. She poured her cherries into Rosie's pail, then went back into the tree to fill her pail again. In an hour or so we walked home, eager to show Mom the pails full of cherries. Rosie presented her pail of cherries to Mom and received praise equal to that of the rest of us. I think of my helpless little sister every time I read Paul's conversation in Romans. "Therefore having been justified by faith, we have peace with God through our Lord Jesus Christ, … and we exult in hope of the glory of God.… And hope does not disappoint, because the love of God has been poured out within our hearts through the Holy Spirit who was given to us. For while we were still helpless, at the right time Christ died for the ungodly" (Rom. 5:1–6).

All of us stand before a holy God with empty pails. We have no righteousness to recommend us. The way to heaven appears an impossible trail that we cannot negotiate on our own feebleness. We can only cry out, as did Isaiah, "Woe is me, I am undone."

But God sees our bankruptcy and our emptiness. He finds a way to fill our emptiness and bring us peace. Taking upon Himself our weakness, He dies the second death for us and lives a life of perfection that He pours into our emptiness. As a result, we stand before the Father dressed in Jesus' holiness—and we are not ashamed. We have the assurance that heaven is our home.

The astounding part of this transaction is that it is a gift. Forgiveness, growth in grace, victory over sin, peace that passes all human understanding—all are gifts.

My father gave me a gift when I left home to go to college. He pulled the gold watch from his pocket, rubbed it carefully with his hands, and said, "Bubs, you'll need to know what time it is when you're in school. This is the watch Mom gave to me when we married. I want you to have it as your very own." I didn't feel that I deserved such kindness, but I knew my father's offer was a gift of love. Taking the watch, I used it for years. Then one day something shattered my heart. A thief broke into our home and stole my watch. That watch was a symbol of my father's love. Now it was gone. That was more than 20 years ago, but I still wish I could have my father's watch.

God's gift of forgiveness and redemption cost Him His Son, yet He freely gave it to us. Wrapped in divine love and bathed in the blood of Golgotha, it is forever a symbol of the incomprehensible and unconditional affection of the Trinity. Satan, the stealthy one, makes every possible attempt to steal our freedom and the gift of forgiveness, but we lay up our treasure in heaven, where no thieves can enter.

Bishop Desmond Tutu expresses our security in God's gift: "What we are, what we have, even our salvation, all is a gift, all is grace, not to be achieved but to be received as a gift freely given. God's bias in favor of sinners is so immense that it is said we will be surprised at those we will find in heaven whom we had not expected to encounter there. Ultimately no one is an irredeemable cause devoid of all hope. No situation in this theology is irredeemable and devoid of hope. God does not give up on anyone, for God loved us from all eternity, God loves us now and God will always love us, all of us good and bad, forever and ever. Someone has said there is nothing I can do to make God love me more, for God loves me perfectly already. And wonderfully, there is nothing I can do to make God love me less. When I realize the deep love God has for me, I will strive for love's sake to do what pleases my Lover" (*No Future Without Forgiveness* [New York: Doubleday, 1999], p. 85). Something profoundly dawned on me when I was helping my young sons make a Christmas gift for their mother. Knowing that she was fond of candles and candleholders, they decided to make a unique candleholder. They asked me to help them. We obtained a nice piece of wood at a building site scrap pile. The boys sanded it smooth. Then they found a piece of driftwood at the beach that we attached to the wooden base. One of the boys had a little porcelain sea gull that he glued to the driftwood. Next we placed a figurine of a retired sea captain beside it. The oldest boy suggested that we fasten a piece of a broom handle in an upright position and then attach a little wooden cup on the top as a candleholder.

On Christmas morning my wife opened the awkwardly wrapped gift. She broke into a big smile and thanked the boys profusely, then placed the candleholder on an end table, where it remained for years. That Christmas morning it dawned on me that givers can be just as excited about a gift as the receiver. They had immense pleasure making the gift and in watching Mom open it.

As I reminisced about that Christmas gift the text in Hebrews 12:1–3 entered my mind. "Therefore, since we have so great a cloud of witnesses surrounding us, let us also lay aside every encumbrance and the sin which so easily entangles us, and let us run with endurance the race that is set before us, fixing our eyes on Jesus, the author and perfecter of faith, who for the joy set before Him endured the cross, despising the shame, and has sat down at the right hand of the throne of God. For consider Him who has endured such hostility by sinners against Himself, so that you will not grow weary and lose heart."

The passage quite plainly says that our redemption is a source of joy to Him. Considering the price paid, I don't comprehend how joy could have been involved, but then I don't fully grasp God's love. Every aspect of preparing and bestowing the gift of forgiveness and salvation brings joy to God. The apostle Paul must have puzzled over this and other aspects of redemption until he finally threw up his hands and cried, "Thanks be to God for His indescribable gift!" (2 Cor. 9:15).

We see the concept of forgiveness and the various dimensions of redemption being a gift throughout Scripture. One of my favorite Pauline passages declares: "If God is for us, who is against us? He who did not spare His own Son, but delivered Him over for us all, how will He not also with Him freely give us all things? Who will bring a charge against God's elect? God is the one who justifies; who is the one who condemns? Christ Jesus is He who died, yes, rather who was raised, who is at the right hand of God, who also intercedes for us.... I am convinced that neither death, nor life, nor angels, nor principalities, nor things present, nor things to come, nor powers, nor height, nor depth, nor any other created thing, shall be able to separate us from the love of God, which is in Christ Jesus our Lord" (Rom. 8:31–39).

God spared no gift to restore His earthly family. He jealously guards His treasured people from the snares of the devil. All who gather under His umbrella of grace to utilize the unconditional gift of forgiveness also receive the power to live victoriously.

A touching story of giving appears in the fourth chapter of John. Jesus' disciples went to town to buy some lunch while He rested by a well. A Samaritan woman came to the well to draw water, and Jesus asked her for a drink. That a Jew would lower himself to speak to a Samaritan puzzled her, but Jesus quickly spoke to her heart. "If you knew the gift of God, and who it is who says to you, 'Give Me a drink,' you would have asked Him, and He would have given you living water…. Everyone who drinks of this water [meaning the well water] will thirst again; but whoever drinks of the water that I will give him shall never thirst; but the water that I will give him will become in him a well of water springing up to eternal life" (verses 10–14).

This Samaritan woman was fortunate to have access to a well. Many people in the region relied on rainwater caught in cisterns. As she conversed with Jesus it was soon apparent to her that Jesus was talking about life free of guilt and shame. She knew Jesus must be the Christ, because He knew her marital status, yet she sensed a forgiving spirit in Him. She returned to her village and let the whole town know about this water-of-life Stranger. Can you imagine the conversations that went buzzing around town about a well of water springing up to eternal life?

I worked one hot summer in southern Ohio selling books. Down along the Ohio River and in the hills overlooking the river very few families had money for a dug well. They caught rainwater coming from the roof and stored it in cisterns. No matter how thirsty I was, I refused to ask for a drink of water from a cistern owner. As summer wore on, many cisterns went dry and the people had to buy water for their cisterns, which meant that they had to take extra precautions when using water for drinking. At several points along the river road pipes emerged from the hillside. Cars lined up to fill gallon jugs with cold spring water that flowed constantly from deep within the ground. It didn't take a chemist to recognize that spring water was superior to stagnant cistern water.

The Samaritan woman immediately realized that what Jesus was offering to give her was superior to the water in the well. She wanted that water. It must have changed her life, yet the water was totally free.

One time I studied the Bible with a factory employee. When we came to what the Bible had to say about forgiveness, I told him that forgiveness was God, just as God is love. I assured him that when he opened his life to the flow of God's forgiveness, it would be as if he had never done anything wrong. The slate is wiped clean. He looked at me with an expression of disbelief and said, "Larry, if that is true, it is the best news I have ever had."

I wish the apostle John had told us more about the Samaritan woman. We can only guess what life must have been like for her after she met Jesus. Much like modern people, she may have felt that she should do something to deserve forgiveness. I hope she finally accepted it as a gift and that she told the inhabitants of her village that it was the best news she had ever had.

What I like about the gift of forgiveness is that it keeps flowing. The well doesn't run dry. You don't have droughts when you have to buy it. It is like the artesian well in the Pigeon River Country State Forest in Michigan. The cold water runs from the spout of an old iron pump. The pump has no handle because the force of the aquifer is so powerful that it propels the water from the spout with amazing pressure. Thus the pump never needs priming. The water flows constantly and is free of charge. My boys and I backpacked in that forest for five summers. We always filled two dozen jugs to use at home.

That artesian well wasn't flowing because we did anything remarkable. Years before we backpacked in that forest, the cold water was quenching the thirst of weary hikers. We didn't deposit money into a slot to get it. The water was a free gift.

Simon, the converted magician, saw the gift of the Holy Spirit changing people when Peter and John ministered in the city of Samaria. The old urge to feel self-important returned and Simon offered to pay money to acquire the power. Peter wasted no time in declaring, "May your silver perish with you, because you thought you could obtain the gift of God with money" (Acts 8:20).

Trying to pay for a gift insults the giver. Imagine a man telling his wife, "Now, save all the receipts from the gifts you give me this year so

I can reimburse you."

She might reply, "No way! My gifts are a sign of my love. You couldn't begin to afford the price of love."

Henri J. M. Nouwen, commenting on the parable of the lost sheep, will probably end any thoughts you might have about earning forgiveness. "It often seems that the more I try to disentangle myself from the darkness, the darker it becomes. I need light, but that light has to conquer my darkness, and that I cannot bring about myself. I cannot forgive myself. I cannot make myself feel loved. By myself I cannot leave the land of my anger. I cannot bring myself home nor can I create communion on my own. I can desire it, hope for it, wait for it, yes, pray for it. But my true freedom I cannot fabricate for myself. That must be given to me. I am lost. I must be found and brought home by the shepherd who goes out to me" (*The Return of the Prodigal Son* [New York: Doubleday, 1994], p. 82).

The gifts of forgiveness, reconciliation, and restoration bring joyful music to heaven. Grand choruses fill it even when only one sinner opens their life to these gifts. The angels in chorus cannot comprehend forgiveness. It is far beyond their ability to plumb the depths of love that stoops to save, but they sing to celebrate God's joy and the joy of the redeemed. Every person who accepts the free gift of forgiveness swells the family of God. The music of heaven marks that increase. The angels rejoice and welcome us.

Their music is praise to the divine Forgiver, not to the wealthy sinner who earned forgiveness, nor to those capable of changing their lives by their own strong will. L. Gregory Jones reminds us that "we are not required to change in order to be forgiven by God; as I have repeatedly insisted, there is nothing we can do to earn that forgiveness. Instead, we are enabled by God to become holy because we have been forgiven" (*Embodying Forgiveness,* p. 184).

The music of heaven glorifies and exalts the One who can remove our robes of failure and folly and dress us in royal garments not of our own making.

The apostle Paul had spent years congratulating himself on living a circumspect life in harmony with the letter of the law. Then he met Jesus. What a difference Christ made in his life. From that point on, Paul called himself the chief of sinners. No more self-congratulation. The gift of God's grace was uppermost in his thinking. In his first letter to the Christians in Corinth he wrote: "I thank my God always concerning you for the grace of God which was given you in Christ Jesus, that in everything you were enriched in Him, in all speech and all knowledge, even as the testimony concerning Christ was confirmed in you, so that you are not lacking in any gift, awaiting eagerly the revelation of our Lord Jesus Christ, who will also confirm you to the end, blameless in the day of our Lord Jesus Christ" (1 Cor. 1:4–8).

When we stand with Paul before God's throne, we will take no credit to ourselves. We will probably say, "I owe it all to Jesus. If it had not been for His gifts, I would not be here." My wife and I attended a gala banquet in Fort Worth, Texas. As we entered the hotel the shimmering beauty of the giant chandeliers startled us. Bubbling fountains sent tiny streams trickling between flowers of all colors of the rainbow. We ascended winding stairs covered with thick rugs and entered a large room with tables covered with rich hors d'oeuvres. Men dressed in tuxedos escorted meticulously coiffured women dressed in silken gowns. Among the guests were professors from Texas Christian University, presidents of large corporations such as Tandy, and executives of large oil companies. I held an animated conversation with a casually dressed man, thinking that he was closer to my socioeconomic class. I later met an acquaintance who knew his way around Dallas-Fort Worth society. He told me, "Larry, that simply dressed fellow you've been chatting with happens to be the third wealthiest man in Dallas-Fort Worth." "Wait a minute, Larry!" you say. "You must be in the upper tax bracket to be mingling with these people." Wrong! You see, attending the banquet was a gift. It didn't cost me a penny.

Soon I shall be seated at the heavenly banquet table hosted by Jesus. The fancy banquet in Fort Worth will be pauper's fare compared to the delicacies served to all the redeemed. From the lips of its guests we will hear such words as "It's really true. Eternity is God's gift to all who opened their hearts to His forgiving grace."

Chapter 5

REPENTANCE—
Opening the Flood Gates of Forgiveness

Miles north of the city of Lebanon, Pennsylvania, lies a reservoir covering hundreds of acres behind a heavy dam. Cold mountain springs feed the reservoir at Highpoint, keeping it full year-round. The excess water spills into a stream that was my father's favorite wading place on a hot Sabbath afternoon. Huge pipes carry water to the city for the residents to drink. The residents simply turn a faucet, and refreshing water flows into their glass.

I sold books one summer in Lebanon. On hot days people shared that water with me. My energy returned and my mood lifted when a resident gladly gave me a glass of cold water.

I met a few people living on the edge of the city who insisted on using their wells, even though the danger of contamination was real. The municipality piped the clear spring water of Highpoint right down their street, but they refused to tap into the line. By their own choice they deprived themselves of safe water and the opportunity to share it with thirsty friends and strangers.

God's forgiveness, like a never-diminishing reservoir, was available long before the foundation of the world as a contingency should the human family ever fall. Instantly He implemented the plan of redemption when we faced death from which we could not deliver ourselves (see 1 Peter 1:19, 20; Matt. 25:34; Eph. 1:4).

The reservoir of forgiveness is not a human-made, human-deserved provision. Forgiveness flows from God's mind and heart. He sends it as a mighty gushing stream into the life of repentant sinners, but the flood of forgiveness does not stop there. It spills over to bless others.

Forgiveness, if it is to bless us, demands a response from us, but it is not one of human effort. Jesus said: "And I, if I am lifted up from the earth, will draw all men to Myself " (John 12:32). Jesus here has in mind His death on the cross. Through the cross Jesus became a magnetic force, attracting sinners. The apostle Paul saw the cross as God's kindness when he said, "The kindness of God leads you to repentance" (Rom. 2:4).

The Holy Spirit empowered the early Christians to proclaim the cross and the empty tomb. People were attracted to the Man who vacated both, and by their faithful teaching and example Christ's followers initiated them into the kingdom of heaven.

The Beatitudes give us fresh insight into repentance and forgiveness. These carefully constructed dimensions of the Christian life are not an ideal to be someday reached in eternity, neither are they optional characteristics of God's children. A complete picture of the person who fully depends on the grace of God, they describe the daily life of His followers. Once I used the study of the Beatitudes as a basis for an evangelistic program. I asked a local artist to paint a 4' x 8' picture that I mounted on the platform. On the left it depicted a barren desert symbolizing life apart from Christ. In the middle was a mountain with lookout towers, three going up the mountain, one at the top, and three descending the mountain. On the right spread a pleasant valley symbolizing life with Christ. The three ascending towers represented self-emptying. The tower at the peak stood for being filled by God's grace. The descending towers depicted the life that overflows with grace to bless others.

The artist attended the meetings. One evening she told me, "I hate to look at that mountain. It discourages me, because I know I can never achieve what it represents."

"That's precisely what I was hoping to convey," I answered. "Forgiveness, repentance, reconciliation, and victorious Christian living are possible only by the power that comes from above. God never asks us to have a relationship with Him without granting us the gift to succeed."

The first beatitude describes the genesis of the Christian life. "Blessed are the poor in spirit, for theirs is the kingdom of heaven" (Matt. 5:3). In my penchant for alphabetizing things, I called this the beatitude of acknowledgment.

As we behold Jesus we begin looking at our own life in a realistic manner. All illusions of self-righteousness evaporate before our eyes. We acknowledge that we are spiritual pygmies standing before our Creator and Redeemer. Our spiritual poverty is so pronounced that we can't deny our need of a Savior.

D. Martyn Lloyd-Jones once said: "If one feels anything in the presence of God save an utter poverty of spirit, it ultimately means that you have never faced Him" (*Studies in the Sermon on the Mount* [Grand Rapids: Eerdmans Pub. House, 1967], p. 45).

Then Lloyd-Jones defines "poor in spirit." "It means a complete absence of pride, a complete absence of self-assurance and of self-reliance. It means a consciousness that we are nothing in the presence of God. It is nothing, then, that we can produce; it is nothing that we can do in ourselves. It is just this tremendous awareness of our utter nothingness as we come face to face with God" (Ibid., p. 50).

Some secular counselors consider an awareness of personal nothingness as unhealthy, but their reaction indicates that they do not understand the way God deals with us. The Lord never reveals our nothingness to leave us in despair. Nor does He allow guilt and spiritual inadequacy to be unaccompanied by hope.

As we study the life of Jesus in the Gospels and acknowledge that we are spiritual paupers in need of forgiveness, we find ourselves drawn by God's compassion and led to repentance. We brokenheartedly confess our sin and understand from experience that "blessed are those who mourn, for they shall be comforted" (verse 4). The beatitude of the brokenhearted promises that we are not left in a hopeless state. The Comforter, God's Spirit, brings assurance that the slate has been wiped clean.

Once we have been emptied of the last vestige of self, it can be said of us, "Blessed are the gentle, for they shall inherit the earth" (verse 5). I like to call this the beatitude of calm. After God takes away all pride and self-importance we no longer have to prove anything to others. All boasting and spiritual unrest are gone. We can relax in the Lord's goodness. In our calmness we become open to receive the many gifts of grace that await us in our journey with God.

Repentance is literally a turning around and going in the right direction. No longer encumbered with the sins of the past, we can enjoy the leading of the Lord. Thus repentance is like opening a faucet in Lebanon, Pennsylvania, to fill a glass with cool water. Judd had this experience.

I had just finished conducting a revival service. The congregation had gone home, and I was gathering my Bible and notes into my briefcase when I heard footsteps in the foyer of the church and saw Judd making his way down the aisle toward me. He appeared troubled and nervous. In a few minutes he told me he had strayed away from the church and God, but something had happened to him at work. Driving a huge truck at a construction site, he often had to wait to load and unload, sometimes 15 minutes. While he waited he noticed a New Testament on the dashboard of his truck. He read it every chance he had. With each reading he felt God speaking to him. That night he knew he had to find peace.

As we knelt in the aisle of the church I invited Judd to pray for forgiveness. After much sobbing, he blurted out, "O God, please help me!" He couldn't speak another word because the sobs came fast and furious. I asked him if he wanted me to finish his prayer, which I did. I told God Judd's story and then asked the Lord to wipe the slate clean for him. Then I thanked God for casting his sins in the depths of the sea and thanked Him for giving Judd peace. The prayer was short. After the tears subsided Judd looked up at me with a smile that grew broader by the second.

That's what repentance is all about. God pipes the water of His forgiveness right down our street. When we respond to God's invitation to repent, peace floods our heart. The peace that passes all human understanding calms us and leaves us receptive to blessings beyond our imagination.

God did not give Judd forgiveness and peace as payment for any merit on his part. As he read the good news from the New Testament on the truck dashboard, the message of the cross drew him to Jesus. He responded to God's love by acknowledging his condition and opening his life to the eternal flood of forgiveness.

Alister E. McGrath stated this process clearly: "One of the most remarkable features of the gospel is the assertion that man is brought to God through God being brought to man. Forgiveness imparts, rather than demands, newness of life. It is the offer of forgiveness, so powerfully and tenderly embodied in the dying incarnate God, Jesus Christ, which brings home to man his need for repentance and amendment. Man can come to God, just as he is, knowing that the offer of pardon and forgiveness carries with it the promise of transformation and renewal" (*Understanding Jesus*, pp. 169, 170).

Something of divine origin was happening in Judd's life long before he walked down the aisle of my church. His repentance had nothing to do with anything I initiated. I simply became a participant in a process that God had already begun.

Robert Shank said: "Not one man ever has turned to God for saving grace except on the basis of the prior initiative and enabling grace of God. And not one man ever has sought God and His saving grace without the deliberate exercise of his own initiative in response to God's gracious initiative" (*Elect in the Son* [Minneapolis: Bethany House Publishers, 1989], p. 204).

Repentance, then, is just as surely a gift as is forgiveness. Yes, it is my response to God's initiative, but the ever-pleading power of the

Holy Spirit enables me to make it.

Henri J. M. Nouwen wrote: "What is so clear is that God is always there, always ready to give and forgive, absolutely independent of our response. God's love does not depend on our repentance or our inner or outer changes" (*The Return of the Prodigal Son*, p. 78).

The apostle Peter, moments after denying his acquaintance with Jesus, looked into Jesus' face and saw forgiveness and love. That prompted his repentance. Forgiveness was his even before his prayer in a secluded place.

Fearful Peter had lingered in the shadows at Jesus' trial. The courage to admit his connection with Jesus escaped him, but he could not escape Jesus' notice of him. In a sense the apostle learned the same lesson that Jonah had. Norman Anthony Peart observed that "God teaches Jonah that not only are his arms too short to box with God but his legs are too tiny to run from God" (*Separate No More* [Grand Rapids: Baker Books, 2000], p. 100).

The suffering Son of God saw Peter warming his hands and may have heard his protestations. One glance at Jesus, and the disciple knew that forgiveness was abundant and about to flood his soul. Jesus hadn't forgotten him for a moment. Although physically he ran away, actually he ran to God, to forgiveness, and toward an exciting future of proclaiming the good news of forgiveness.

This takes us back to the beatitude of acknowledgment. By beholding God's untiring patience and love, by meditating on the cross and the empty tomb, and by standing in the awesome presence of our Holy God, we cry out in repentance our spiritual poverty and open ourselves to His rich grace.

The Beatitudes do not describe a static experience. Every day we can behold the crucified and risen Christ through the study of Scripture. Daily we find ourselves baffled by One dying for all. We can continually be moved by the unconditional forgiveness of God, and daily repent and confess our spiritual poverty. Every day we can exclaim, "Thank You, God, for Your generous forgiveness. Thank You for the calming of your presence in my life."

Forgiveness and repentance go hand in hand. They are a work in progress, fitting us for eternal fellowship with the great Forgiver.

Dietrich Bonhoeffer wrote: "The prodigal in Luke 15, who knows himself to be lost, is accepted again by the father. That is to say, the one who is ready to repent finds forgiveness. Penitence and forgiveness are so closely tied that one can reverse the principle: only he who is forgiven finds his way to penitence. Only he who is penitent receives the kingdom of heaven, and only because the kingdom of heaven has come near is there repentance" (*Spiritual Care* [Fortress Press, 1985], p. 44).

Commenting on the woman who bathed Jesus' feet with tears and perfume (Luke 7), L. Gregory Jones makes these insightful observations: "The story has sometimes been taken as an indication that people can earn forgiveness through repentance. But on closer examination, it shows that God's forgiveness induces her repentance of showing extravagant love. She has not earned her forgiveness through the repentance of extravagant love; because she has been forgiven, she is able to repent by showing such love. The woman's extravagant love shows both the transformative power of forgiveness and the specific patterns of repentance enabled by that forgiveness" (*Embodying Forgiveness*, pp. 160–162).

The longer we behold the crucified, risen, and soon coming Lord, the clearer become the implications of our waywardness. It means that repentance will be an ongoing process, a daily indicator that the floodgates of forgiveness have opened, spilling into our lives, then into the lives of those around us.

As long as we live, the Christian journey will find us repeatedly at the foot of the cross where we have an ongoing appropriation of forgiveness and an ongoing call to repentance. I learned that when I was baptized at 12.

My family and I drove 100 miles to Chestertown, Maryland, for the baptism. I vowed that I would not quarrel with my sisters over who was hogging more than their share of the back seat. During the round trip I succeeded. I was happy about this because I had confessed my quarrelsome nature to God, received His forgiveness, and now He gave me the victory.

When we arrived home my father stopped the car at the end of the long farm lane. There sat the F-20 Farmall tractor with four empty milk cans on the platform bolted to the drawbar. The creamery truck driver had taken the full cans and left the empties. "Bubs, start the tractor," my father said to me, "and drive it up to the milk house." I hated to crank the tractor, because when I didn't do it correctly the crank sometimes struck me on the head. In a flash I replied in a sassy voice, "I'm not going to do it!"

When I heard my father's second command I knew that I didn't dare refuse again. I started the motor and climbed behind the wheel. Suddenly it struck me. Although baptized just that day, I had already disobeyed. With tears streaming down my face I cried to the Lord, "O God, if I'm going to live for You, You'll have to help me. Please forgive me for sassing my father."

I parked the F-20 and slowly entered the stable where I apologized to my father. He assured me that he had forgiven me. "That's all right, Bubs. You're a good boy."

Never after that did he remind me of the offense.

I learned that day that God has a habit of forgiving and that repentance is an ongoing gift that keeps my relationship with God joyful.

Chapter 6

FORGIVENESS—
Wrapped With Divine Power

The fast-approaching Christmas season sent my wife and me to the toy section of a department store. Our goal was to find a remote-controlled car for each of our two grandsons. We settled on two sleek models within our price range. My wife wrapped them with flashy paper and placed them under the Christmas tree.

On Christmas morning the boys ripped the paper from their packages and promptly attempted to operate their cars. The first boy soon maneuvered his car around the torn gift wrap lying on the living room floor, but the second boy couldn't make his car run. His father picked up the box it came in and read the fine print: "Power pack not included." My heart went out to Eric. A car with no power! How could I have overlooked the notice on the box? A week later I found a store that sold the right power pack. Now both boys race their cars on their driveway.

When God's forgiveness floods our life, it is more than a legal transaction. His forgiveness comes with a power pack-none other than the Holy Spirit. Power to live for God in the present and the future always accompanies deliverance from a faulty past.

The apostle Paul spoke much about power. "For this reason I bow my knees before the Father, from whom every family in heaven and on earth derives its name, that He would grant you, according to the riches of His glory, to be strengthened with power through His Spirit in the inner man, so that Christ may dwell in your hearts through faith; and that you, being rooted and grounded in love, may be able to comprehend with all the saints what is the breadth and length and height and depth, and to know the love of Christ which surpasses knowledge, that you may be filled up to all the fullness of God. Now to Him who is able to do exceeding abundantly beyond all that we ask or think, according to the power that works within us, to Him be the glory in the church and in Christ Jesus to all generations forever and ever. Amen" (Eph. 3:14–21).

"Finally, be strong in the Lord and in the strength of His might. Put on the full armor of God, so that you will be able to stand firm against the schemes of the devil" (Eph. 6:10,11).

"I am not ashamed of the gospel, for it is the power of God for salvation to everyone who believes, to the Jew first and also to the Greek. For in it the righteousness of God is revealed from faith to faith; as it is written, 'But the righteous man shall live by faith'" (Rom. 1:16, 17).

As a teenager I struggled with how to live a victorious life. Quite frankly, I was trying to do it with my own power. While taking my ninth grade of school by correspondence, I read this arresting statement by Ellen G. White: "Christ has made every provision for us to be strong. He has given us His Holy Spirit, whose office is to bring to our remembrance all the promises that Christ made, that we may have peace and a sweet sense of forgiveness. If we will but keep our eyes fixed on the Saviour, and trust in His power, we shall be filled with a sense of security; for the righteousness of Christ will become our righteousness" (*Messages to Young People* [Nashville: Southern Pub. Assn., 1930], p. 107).

The "sweet sense of forgiveness" meant to me that I didn't have to fret about how I would live after forgiveness, because along with it came God's power.

The apostle Paul focused on his own weaknesses at one point. He even prayed about them. The Lord told him, "My grace is sufficient for you, for power is perfected in weakness" (2 Cor. 12:9). In response to God's message, Paul said, "I am well content with weaknesses, with insults, with distresses, with persecutions, with difficulties, for Christ's sake; for when I am weak, then I am strong" (verse 10).

An intern pastor and I visited a church member who had been active in church activities for many years. She spent a long time recounting her weaknesses and expressing doubts of ever making it to heaven. The intern finally interrupted her litany.

"Eleanor, you remind me of a story about a vacuum cleaner salesman. This salesman asked permission to demonstrate his vacuum for Mrs. Jones. Once inside her house, the salesman threw a little bag of dirt on Mrs. Jones's new white rug. Then he pushed the attachment over the rug, only to drive the dirt into her new rug. Mrs. Jones promptly asked him to leave.

"An hour later another vacuum cleaner salesman rang the doorbell at Mrs. Jones's house. After much convincing, he was allowed into the living room. He unwrapped the power cord, plugged it into the outlet, then threw a bag of dirt on the white rug. Slowly he ran the attachment over the area of the rug where both bags of dirt had been emptied. Instantly the dirt was gone. Mrs. Jones could not tell where the dirt had been. She bought the vacuum. Now, Eleanor, what was the difference between the two salesmen?"

She thought for a moment and said, "Why, that first fellow never plugged his machine into the outlet!"

The intern gently said, "Eleanor, I think you are like the first salesman. You are concentrating on the dirt, the weaknesses of your life. You need to focus on God's power."

Eleanor had prayed many times about her weaknesses. She longed to be ready to meet Jesus, but she forgot to give priority to God's power. The woman had lost sight of the fact that God's forgiveness comes wrapped in divine power. Max Lucado commented, "Righteousness. That's it. That's what we are thirsty for. We're thirsty for a clean conscience. We crave a clean slate. We yearn for a fresh start. We pray for a hand which will enter the dark cavern of our world and do for us the one thing we can't do for ourselves-make us right again" (*The Applause of Heaven* [Dallas: Word Publishing, 1996], p. 86).

Forgiveness that simply erases the past is not the complete gift. God steps into our life with power to make us right again. The apostle Paul spoke with assurance when he said, "I am confident of this very thing, that He who began a good work in you will perfect it until the day of Christ Jesus" (Phil. 1:6).

The good work that God does in us begins much earlier than we realize. The magnetic pull of the cross tugs at us while we are still rebelling. When we eventually open ourselves to His forgiving grace, we join in the efforts to grow to Christian maturity. Linked with God's power, we find transformation taking place in our lives.

God uses many ways to tip the scale in favor of repentance and reconciliation. A young woman in Canada lived next to a Seventh-day Adventist church. Every week she heard happy singing. God planted in her heart a thirst for joy. One day she gathered the courage to attend the church, in which she found a supportive and loving community.

A young man visited the library in his city. There he devoured a book about Jesus—*The Desire of Ages*. His life changed as he beheld Jesus in that book.

An agnostic blue-collar worker took a young Christian sightseeing in his small plane. He was so impressed with the gentle ways of his passenger that he became interested in the young man's faith. "That young man did what no older person could have done," he told others. God used his passenger to lead him to repentance and reconciliation with God. I have watched the power of God at work in troubled marriages and unhappy homes. When forgiveness penetrates proud hearts, it can reverse divorce plans. It can eliminate jealousy and destructive competition among siblings. The promise "I am going to send you Elijah the prophet before the coming of the great and terrible day of the Lord. He will restore the hearts of the fathers to their children and the hearts of the children to their fathers" (Mal. 4:5, 6) can be fulfilled. Forgiveness and power can turn a chaotic family system into a little heaven on earth.

My older brothers were obsessed with power when they were young. They tinkered with the timing and carburetor on every car they owned, attempting to increase acceleration.

My father repaired cars from Model T's to later models of the 1950s. He had a unique test for power. If his car could climb the mountain road to Mount Gretna in high gear, he knew he had a powerful car. When my brother bragged about how powerful his car was, my father jumped into the passenger's seat and invited him to take the Mount Gretna hill in high gear. After my brother had to shift down to second gear, rather than admit to lack of power he went back to tinkering with the motor.

In the Christian life we can do without high-powered cars, but we need all the power we can get to escape the corruption of our wicked world. Fortunately the power that accompanies forgiveness has no limit. The apostle Peter said: "His divine power has given us everything we need for life and godliness through our knowledge of him who called us by his own glory and goodness. Through these he has given us his very great and precious promises, so that through them you may participate in the divine nature and escape the corruption in the world caused by evil desires" (2 Peter 1:3, 4, NIV).

This is good news! Forgiveness is not simply release from the past—it is power for the present and the future. And it is available to all God's children, not just a select few. My college roommate was built like a Mack truck. He told me that I could develop huge muscles just like his if I would work out with free weights. So I went to the weight room with him during most of a school year. He increased in bulk, but I was still the same size. All my efforts to become a Mr. Universe were for naught.

I learned later that some people are gifted with muscles that bulge, while others have the lean muscles of a marathon runner.

God's power is equally available to all who are open to the forgiving grace of God. You never receive one without the other. Power is yours because Christ is your strength.

When I was a boy on the farm, making hay required the help of the whole family. We stored loose hay in the lofts of our German bank barn. I wanted the job of pulling the bull rope back to the barn after the tractor towed it into the field. Pulling the rope raised the large fork full of hay from the wagon to the loft, but the rope had to be returned in preparation for the next load.

When extended to the farthest point, the rope was very heavy, but I bragged to my sisters that I was capable of handling it. Grabbing the rope, I tugged valiantly. Surprisingly, I moved it with great ease. Pride swelled in my heart and I looked at my sisters for approval, but they only grinned. That's when I sensed the presence of someone behind me. I looked over my shoulder and saw my strong father hauling in the rope with me.

Many times when faced with difficulties I have thought of my father pulling most of the weight. How much like the Lord he was. When I find the tasks of life beyond my power, He gives me all the strength I need. He uses His power to augment my feeble efforts. Sometimes it seems that God is doing all the pulling.

The apostle Paul wrote: "No temptation has overtaken you but such as is common to man; and God is faithful, who will not allow you to be tempted beyond what you are able, but with the temptation will provide the way of escape also, that you will be able to endure it" (1 Cor. 10:13).

I am encouraged by Eugene Peterson's paraphrase of this passage. After relating the failure of our spiritual forebears, he says: "We are just as capable of messing it up as they were. Don't be so naive and self-confident. You're not exempt. You could fall flat on your face as easily as anyone else. Forget about self-confidence; it's useless. Cultivate God-confidence. No test or temptation that comes your way is beyond the course of what others have had to face. All you need to remember is that God will never let you down; he'll never let you be pushed past your limit; he'll always be there to help you come through it" (verses 12, 13, Message).

My grandson Eric loves to go to summer camp with his parents. He calls it his camp. When he was 6 years old he attempted the ropes course. Of course, he was equipped with a harness to which a long rope was attached. A trained overseer held the rope at all times. Eric told me, "Grandpa, I did fine until near the end. I was too scared to go any farther. And you know how I got off the rope? The man told me to step off the rope. I did. And you know what? The man holding the other rope gently lowered me to the ground. Next year I'll be old enough to go the rest of the way. I don't have to be scared, because someone always has hold of the rope."

Eric preached a good sermon, don't you think? When God forgives us, we set out on a rope course fraught with great challenges, but Someone is always holding the rope. That Someone has all the power we need for a godly life. If we ever reach a point beyond our limit, He will gently deliver us by His mighty grace.

Forgiveness is a work in progress because God never slumbers. He is like artists who keep scrutinizing their canvases and enhance their pictures by little dabs of paint here and there. And He is like authors who edit and reedit their manuscripts until they are just the way they want them to be.

Chapter 7

FORGIVENESS—
Incentive for Obedience

Every Tuesday morning I told stories to the children attending a small church school. One morning as I left the building I encountered a first grader heading toward it. When she saw me she began weeping. Between deep sobs she cried, "I missed it! I missed it!"

I assured her she had not missed school, because classes had just begun. "No," she cried, "I missed the story. Oh, I missed the story!"

Squatting down to her level, I squeezed her little hands and said, "That's all right, Christine. I know it's not your fault for getting to school late. Now, don't cry. I will get permission from your teacher to tell the story tomorrow morning. I'll tell it just for you."

Christine was waiting for me the next morning. I took her to an empty room and related the story she had missed. Sending her back to her classroom, I then headed for my car until I heard a little voice behind me. "Pastor, wait-wait!" I turned and saw Christine running toward me. Once again I squatted to her level. She reached out, opened one of my hands, and slipped something into it. "Pastor, I want you to have this as your very own."

When I opened my hand I saw a quarter. It was Christine's milk money for the week. My first impulse was to thank her, but urge her to keep it. Then I realized that I was looking at a gift of love straight from the heart of a thankful child. "Oh, Christine! Thank you very much. I will always treasure this gift."

Christine returned to her classroom, and I drove away a happy man. When school dismissed and the students were gone, I paid for Christine's milk, but I kept her quarter as a reminder of my self-sacrificing, grateful little friend.

I think of Christine many times when I study the topic of forgiveness. We frequently miss the mark and run to God crying, "Oh, Lord, I'm sorry for coming up short and tripping over my own feet. Please forgive me for not living for You today." Then we realize that God came to earth to die and save sinners even if only one of His children had missed the mark. He stooped and looked at us on our level in order to give us the gift of forgiveness wrapped in power. Our hearts are broken as we acknowledge our spiritual poverty, but God wipes the slate clean and endows us with the desire and the strength to walk with Him in obedience.

Our obedience doesn't begin to purchase forgiveness. It is a mere quarter, but it represents a self-sacrificing, grateful heart, an act of appreciation for a gift we don't deserve. One theologian observed: "A life of obedience to God is the fruit of fait…. It springs from gratitude for grace received, not from the desire to gain merit and to justify oneself in God's sight" (J. D. Douglas, ed., *The New Bible Dictionary* [Grand Rapids: Eerdmans Pub. Co., 1962], p. 904).

One time I spent an entire afternoon searching for the home of a Bible correspondence school graduate. He lived on a remote dirt road near the Ohio River. Because he had requested a visit, I anticipated an uplifting conversation. Early in the visit he proceeded to tell me that God's law had been done away with when Jesus died on the cross. He spoke so rapidly that I couldn't get a word in, so I just listened until he tired.

I told him that the book of Galatians teaches that obedience of law-any law-could not earn eternal life because it is a gift from God. Trying to gain heaven by obedience is like trying to lift yourself by your own bootstraps. Obedience, I told him, is an outward manifestation of the inward work of the Holy Spirit. Love invades the human heart, enabling the forgiven sinner to obey as an act of gratitude and worship. Such obedience is evidence that we are saved, not a means of earning eternal life.

I shared the words of John. "For this is the love of God, that we keep His commandments; and His commandments are not burden-some" (1 John 5:3). First comes God's love, which imparts forgiveness and power, then obedience is our joyous response.

The apostle Peter wrote: "He Himself bore our sins in His body on the cross, so that we might die to sin and live to righteousness; for by His wounds you were healed" (1 Peter 2:24). Living a righteous life occurs through God's grace in appreciation for the cross.

The apostle Paul said: "For it is God who is at work in you, both to will and to work for His good pleasure" (Phil. 2:13).

Eugene Peterson's paraphrase of this passage reads: "Be energetic in your life of salvation, reverent and sensitive before God. That energy is God's energy, an energy deep within you, God himself willing and working at what will give him the most pleasure" (Message).

Perhaps the most concise rendering of Philippians 2:12, 13 is: "Keep on working with fear and trembling to complete your salvation, because God is always at work in you to make you willing and able to obey his own purpose" (TEV). An elderly Texas pecan farmer pre-scribed a cure for my puny little pecan trees that had remained two feet high for several years. "Come spring when the ground is soft, poke 10 or 12 holes two feet deep around the drip line. Fill each hole with high-nitrogen fertilizer, then step back and watch 'em grow." He chuckled as he dumped 20 pounds of pecans in a bag for me.

For the next four years I followed his advice. At the end of the four years the trees were as high as the house roof.

The high nitrogen of the Holy Spirit comes with the gift of forgive-ness, prompting growth in obedience. The apostle Paul advises us to "be transformed by the renewing of your mind, so that you may prove what the will of God is, that which is good and acceptable and perfect" (Rom. 12:2). In Titus 3:5 he indicates that the Holy Spirit is the renewing agent, the nitrogen of growth, if you please.

L. William Countryman presents an exciting idea: "Being forgiven isn't the last step in a process, then, as if being forgiven settled everything. We are constantly creating ourselves and our world, and the process is a gradual one. Forgiveness makes it safe to begin changing and growing. It releases possibilities that would otherwise remain locked away" (*Forgiven and Forgiving* [Harrisburg, Pa: Morehouse Publishing, 1998], p. 40).

Theologians often use the word "sanctification" to describe the releasing and actualizing of possibilities that forgiveness sets in motion. Forgiven people conceive and put into operation all sorts of creative and innovative approaches to advancing God's kingdom.

In a previous chapter we referred to the first three beatitudes. We acknowledge our spiritual poverty, confess our waywardness, then rejoice in the peace that comes through forgiveness. This begins a continual desire for more of God's grace and a willingness to share the good news of forgiveness with others. It is not a static experience, but a way of life. Daily we empty all vestiges of self, receive the growth-inducing grace of God, and reach out to others.

You could describe this as a bonding with Christ that takes place after our deliverance from the bondage of sin. Israel exchanged bondage in Egypt for bonding with God. The law written on stone, a reflection of God's character, He intended to be written in the lives of His people with the ink of the Holy Spirit, but Israel was not receptive to the divine penmanship. But the heavenly Scribe persisted, and today "the same law that was engraved upon the tables of stone is written by the Holy Spirit upon the tables of the heart. Instead of going about to establish our own righteousness we accept the righteousness of Christ. His blood atones for our sins. His obedience is accepted for us. Then the heart renewed by the Holy Spirit will bring forth 'the fruits of the Spirit.' Through the grace of Christ we will live in obedience to the law of God written upon our hearts. Having the Spirit of Christ, we shall walk even as He walked" (Ellen G. White, *Patriarchs and Prophets* [Mountain View, Calif.: Pacific Press Pub. Assn., 1913], p. 372).

We can misunderstand the phrase "walk even as He walked." My son and I followed a guide through Wells Gray Provincial Park in British Columbia. He led us up a mountain from the top of which we hoped to see the spray of Helmcken Falls. At first we tried to match the pace of the guide, but I finally had to stop and catch my breath. I pretended to take pictures of wildflowers rather than admit my lack of conditioning. When I finally reached the top, the guide apologized for his rapid pace at such a high altitude. My son later admitted that even he could barely keep up.

Following Jesus' pace can be a grueling experience if we attempt it without the Spirit-provided stamina. He never intended that we should walk as He did in our own strength. Israel made that mistake when God gave the guide of life from Sinai. Some still make that error today.

The words translated "trust" and "obey" are closely related. The difference in meaning implies that trust produces obedience (W. F. Vine, *An Expository Dictionary of Biblical Words* [New York: Thomas Nelson Publishers, 1985], p. 438).

I believe that trust is a prerequisite to true obedience, a principle demonstrated every spring on our farm. Starlings built a nest in the mechanism that permitted the fork full of loose hay to travel across the track attached to the peak of the barn. My father asked me to climb the extension ladder and remove the nest. We fully extended the ladder and placed it perpendicular to the middle of the barn floor. My father and older brother steadied the ladder as I scrambled up to the peak. As you might have suspected, I was the youngest and the featherweight of the boys. "You don't need to worry," my father told me. "We won't let it fall." I promptly obeyed my father's request, never doubting their ability to keep the ladder upright. Why? I trusted their strength. I trusted because I had observed their strong arms and seen them lift far more than I could.

Obeying God is not burdensome, but a pleasure-when we trust God completely. We develop such trust by being acquainted with God. This happens by studying the Bible, observing nature, experiencing God's providence and seeing it at work in the lives of others, and praying and meditating on God's love. Trust develops also as we open our lives to God's forgiveness, peace, and power.

My family moved to a farm in southern Pennsylvania after the barn burned down at the one farther north where my father was a sharecropper. The Christians who met in a log-cabin home every Sabbath eased our grief over the experience. A man by the name of Frank Bullock drove many miles from the Eastern Shore of Maryland to lead our small group. Once a week Frank gathered the young people in his car and took us to assist in giving Bible studies to neighboring families. Our role was to sing the songs that appeared on the filmstrips. One of my favorites was "Trust and Obey."

> "When we walk with the Lord
> In the light of His word,
> What a glory He sheds on our way!
> While we do His good will,
> He abides with us still,
> And with all who will trust and obey.
> Trust and obey, for there's no other way
> To be happy in Jesus,
> But to trust and obey."

No, forgiveness is not the last word. By the power of the Holy Spirit we find ourselves transformed by the renewing of our minds. Our gratitude swells the more we know God. Joyous obedience results. We are happy in Jesus.

The apostle John summed it up beautifully. "My little children, I am writing these things to you so that you may not sin. And if anyone sins, we have an Advocate with the Father, Jesus Christ the righteous; and He Himself is the propitiation for our sins; and not for ours only, but also for those of the whole world. By this we know that we have come to know Him, if we keep His commandment....

Whoever keeps His word, in him the love of God has truly been perfected" (1 John 2:1–5).

I grew up hearing pastors and evangelists saying that obedience to the law of God, especially the Sabbath commandment, is a sign of one's loyalty to God. They taught that Sabbath is a test of obedience. While I would not totally disagree, I maintain that the law of God, and the Sabbath in particular, have an even deeper significance.

Similarities between forgiveness and Sabbath are quite remarkable. Forgiveness seeks to release us from the bondage of sin and to set us on the road to restoration by breaking the alienation between us, God, and others. Scripture refers to it as reconciliation and the restoration of God's image in us. Thus forgiveness allows us to walk in harmony with the Lord and others. It involves resting from our own ways so that we can rest in the holiness of Christ. Along with forgiveness come the desire and the strength to walk as Jesus did.

A review of what Sabbath signifies in Scripture shows parallels to forgiveness. After God created the world, He set aside the seventh day as a memorial of His creation. The Sabbath would remind generation after generation that He had created us for a divine purpose.

When God gave the commandments to Israel from Sinai, He said, "I am the Lord your God, who brought you out of the land of Egypt, out of the house of slavery" (Ex. 20:2). Scripture associates deliverance from sin and restoration with the giving of the law, a connection especially interesting, as it pertains to Sabbath.

In the heart of the Ten Commandments is the Sabbath, which yields adoration, worship, and loyalty to the Creator-God as well as respect, honesty, and love toward others.

Later God told Israel that Sabbath should remind them that He was the one who sanctified them. Sanctification is simply God bringing us more and more into a trusting relationship with God (see Eze. 20:12).

The supreme passages about Sabbath appear in Isaiah 58:13, 14. The prophet declares that if we call Sabbath a delight instead of delighting ourselves, we will delight in the Lord. From joyous communion with God would come material, spiritual, and physical blessings unique to God's people.

Jesus entered a world that had buried Sabbath under harsh traditions and prohibitions. In His three-year ministry He demonstrated that it was a time for healing, for life, and for sweet reunion. Sabbath, to Jesus, was a gift to the human family designed to break the bondage of sin and to create bonding with God.

When the Lord of the Sabbath spends holy time with us, the grandeur of His character illuminates the dark places of our hearts and breaks down walls of resistance that we have unwittingly allowed to stand. He creates within us a transparency that prompts a cry from the depths of our soul. "Search me, O God, and know my heart; try me and know my anxious thoughts; and see if there be any hurtful way in me, and lead me in the everlasting way" (Ps. 139:23, 24).

Sabbath is time in which the Lord refurbishes the life and furnishes it with lasting joy. As a result, we make a difference in our world because we have spent time with Him. The gift of forgiveness and the power to obey open all these Sabbath blessings to us. Both forgiveness and Sabbath obedience lead us to spiritual maturity and ultimately to eternal Sabbath rest.

My neighbor and I have similar backgrounds. The man is a farmer, and I grew up on a farm. He farms exclusively with horses, and I worked my father's fields with horses for the better part of a year. And he and his wife have 10 children, while I came from a family of 14. Both of us learned some things about farming the hard way.

During the middle of haying season he asked me to take him to the farm machinery store to purchase a part for his "haybind" that had broken while his son was cutting hay. As we drove to town he told me how it happened.

"When I was using it I noticed that the belt was worn. It caused the propeller to chatter when the hay was thick. If I stopped briefly, the hay wouldn't get jammed in the rollers. My son didn't have the experience with equipment that I did. He kept going when the hay jammed.

I think that caused the breakdown, but that's a good way for a young fellow to learn."

His forgiving attitude toward his son impressed me.

A week after the machine broke I took his son to the hospital with a ruptured appendix. A few days after I brought him home I stopped to see how he was feeling. The boy was weak and had lost 20 pounds. Sitting by an open window, he could hear the sounds of his father and brothers making hay. I could tell that despite his physical condition he longed to be at the barn helping his father with the hay. He wanted to serve a father who had forgiven him an expensive mistake.

People healed and forgiven by Jesus had the same desire to serve. The demoniac, for instance, begged to go with Him, but Jesus commanded him to stay with those he knew and tell what had happened to him. Later Jesus returned to the Decapolis and found many eager listeners, thanks to the obedience and service of the healed demoniac. Forgiveness and restoration were incentives to obey.

One term that Scripture uses for the concept of "to obey" consists of two words—"to listen" and "under." "In the Bible, obedience takes the form of listening. The obedient life is one in which Israel listens to, attends to, and responds to the voice of God" (Walter Brueggemann, *Finally Comes the Prophet* [Minneapolis: Fortress Press, 1989], p. 81).

God designed Sabbath to deliver us from commerce, competition, self-sufficiency, self-control, the culture of greed, and the drive to acquire more and more material possessions. It is a time to silence the noise of the secular so that we can listen to God's voice.

Attending to the voice of God is particularly difficult for us when He speaks in commands. Like my Bible correspondence school student, we rationalize and minimize the importance of the law. Brueggemann says: "Popular religion in our midst has greatly reduced the notion of obedience, so that it has become either a virtue too much celebrated or a burden too much dreaded" (Ibid., p. 80).

Henri J. M. Nouwen said that modern people are afraid of silence. Perhaps we do not dare risk hearing the quiet voice of God lest it challenge our lifestyle.

But forgiven sinners rejoice over leaving behind their noisy and cluttered lives. They listen for the voice of God and are eager to respond, knowing that His commands are not heavy-handed coercion, but a gift that makes wholeness possible. Such individuals don't consider them as dread censure or world-denying prohibition. The voice of God opens windows to new vistas of genuine pleasure.

Listening to, attending to, and responding to God's voice—what a positive way to look at obedience! The question to ask is How can we maximize the experience of all three?

My sisters and I loved to splash in the Swatara Creek that bordered our farm near Lickdale, Pennsylvania. We learned to hold our breath underwater, enabling us to play a simple game. I'd tap two rocks together below the surface while my sisters would drift underwater with the current. The farther downstream they went, the fainter grew the tapping. When they could no longer hear the sound, they would stand up. While it was a game to us, I suppose it was a primitive form of an audiogram. Later in life our simple game became a lesson in obedience for me.

The closer I am to Jesus, the easier it is to hear Him, to attend to His words, and to respond to His will for my life. When I distance myself from Jesus for any reason, my obedience wavers and my joy is not complete.

When the streams of God's refreshing and renewing forgiveness cleanse me every day, I receive strength to remain by His side where I can listen, attend, and respond. In His presence I have peace and fullness of joy.

Chapter 8

FORGIVENESS—
Incentive for Worship

Imagine yourself barging, uninvited, into a party to worship and wash the feet of a special guest with perfume. The din of many voices ceases and all eyes fix on you. To make matters worse, the host loudly objects to what you are doing, yet you continue to kneel at the feet of the guest. You would have to have a good reason for doing such a thing.

The woman who worshiped Jesus in this manner had been forgiven much. Her never-ending gratitude demanded expression, even at the price of embarrassment and open scorn.

Sinners who are astonished at God's mercy and goodness will worship Him continually. They will extol His forgiving grace, even in the face of ridicule.

The Old Testament book of Psalms is a collection of prayers and hymns. They demonstrate the close relationship between forgiveness and worship.

"Pardon my iniquity, for it is great" (Ps. 25:11).

"For You, Lord, are good, and ready to forgive" (Ps. 86:5).

"Bless the Lord, O my soul, and forget none of His benefits; who pardons all your iniquities, who heals all your diseases" (Ps. 103:2, 3).

"There is forgiveness with You" (Ps. 130:4).

"How blessed is he whose transgression is forgiven, whose sin is covered!" (Ps. 32:1).

Worship in the ancient tabernacle centered around forgiveness of sin. A humble and contrite spirit along with the appropriate sacrifice constituted worship for Israel. Almost the entire Old Testament book of Leviticus deals with sacrifice and forgiveness.

Israel left the bondage of Egypt and received an invitation to bond with their Deliverer. A very important part of that bonding took place in worship. Bonding with God requires listening, attending, and responding to His voice. While it happens in personal encounters, corporate worship draws worshipers close to God in a unique manner.

The psalmists understood the value of corporate worship, a fact reflected in their worship songs.

"Let them give thanks to the Lord for His lovingkindness, and for His wonders to the sons of men! Let them extol Him also in the congregation of the people" (Ps. 107:31, 32).

"Praise the Lord! I will give thanks to the Lord with all my heart, in the company of the upright and in the assembly" (Ps. 111:1).

"I will tell of Your name to my brethren; in the midst of the assembly I will praise You" (Ps. 22:22).

"I will give You thanks in the great congregation; I will praise You among a mighty throng" (Ps. 35:18).

"Praise the Lord! Sing to the Lord a new song, and His praise in the congregation of the godly ones" (Ps. 149:1).

The writer of Hebrews reveals that worship is equally important to our spiritual well-being since the cross.

"Let us hold fast the confession of our hope without wavering, for He who promised is faithful; and let us con- sider how to stimulate one another to love and good deeds, not forsaking our own assembling together, as is the habit of some, but encouraging one another; and all the more, as you see the day drawing near" (Heb. 10:23–25).

Forgiveness today, as in the time of Israel, prompts our worship. C. Raymond Holmes wrote: "In worship the church does not celebrate its humanity or its unity or its sanctification or its mission. It celebrates the presence of God and the Lamb. Man is not called to glorify man. Rather, God declares man's worth by His incarnation and Christ's sacrificial act of atonement. It is this fact-that God loved His people so much that He was willing to die for them-that evokes wonder and praise in worship" (*Sing a New Song!* [Berrien Springs, Mich.: Andrews University Press, 1984], p. 20).

Love and forgiveness received as a gift makes a person wonder and even question, especially when the gift is not deserved or earned. Years ago I read about a young Jewish woman imprisoned by the Nazis and assigned to an ammunition plant. Forced to work on an assembly line without adequate nourishment, she constantly fought collapse. When her shift ended she returned to her bunk and wept herself to sleep.

One day she noticed a young mechanic stopping by her conveyor belt. He looked into her eyes intently for a few seconds, then went his way. Before quitting time she noticed a small package about an inch square coming down the belt. She quickly snatched it and dropped it into her apron pocket. That evening as she lay on her bunk she opened the tiny package. Inside was a lump of cheese. The inside of the wrapper bore the words "I love you." Day after day the mechanic would pause and look into her eyes. And day after day she ate a lump of cheese and read the same warm words.

The end of the war freed her, but a few yards from the factory she fainted and fell. When she awakened she found herself surrounded by the sterile walls of a hospital. There she spent many weeks tottering on the brink of death.

The young mechanic visited hospital after hospital, going from room to room looking for the recipient of his cheese and words of love. When he found her she recognized his face. Eagerly she asked, "Why did you share your cheese with me?"

"Because I love you and want to marry you," he replied. After much persuasion she agreed to go to his mother's home where she could fully recover under her skilled care. During her convalescence she struggled with disbelief. *How could anyone love a thin, emaciated creature like me?* she thought.

In time, compelled by the love that she did not think she deserved, she accepted the young mechanic's proposal and ever after lived with gratitude in her heart for her husband.

Forgiven sinners permeated by the grace of God sometimes have to pinch themselves to believe they have really been redeemed. It is good news that takes time to assimilate, but once the reality of eternal life dawns, they love to worship their Savior. They never tire of lifting their hearts and voices in praise and thanksgiving to their merciful Lord. As I wrote the last paragraph, a robin helped to illustrate it. The bird perched on the edge of the birdbath outside my study window. Repeatedly it would look at the fresh water, then turn away. I imagined that it couldn't believe such a luxury was at its disposal. Finally the robin stepped into the water, but splashed only a second before hopping back to the edge of the bath. The second time into the water, though, it made the water fly. Eight times in rapid succession it entered the water and splashed gloriously until it had thoroughly soaked its feathers. Clumsily it flew to a nearby log to dry in the sun.

As I observed the robin Psalm 34:8 came to my mind. "O taste and see that the Lord is good; how blessed is the man who takes refuge in Him!". My feathery friend hesitated at first, but once it felt the cooling water its reluctance disappeared. If it had been human, I suspect it would have come to my windowsill and bowed gratefully.

We taste the forgiveness of God every day. Again and again we return to let the water of God's forgiveness cleanse us. Constantly we bow before Him in worship and praise.

A number of years ago I attended a lectureship on preaching presented by Norval Pease. Speaking on worship, he expressed the desire to see worship streamlined to capture the hearts of modern people, but he didn't linger on the details of what a worship service should be. Instead, he insisted that worship is what happens when a person is willing to be confronted by what God has done, is doing, and will do. Standing in the presence of our holy God, we see our own nature in bold relief. We bow in contrition and amazement at the majesty and glory of the One who has made us, sustains us, and redeems us.

Recently I took my place in the Battle Creek Tabernacle after the service of foot washing. As I sat there I looked at the large picture of Jesus and the rich young ruler on the front wall. Whispering the words to the old hymns being played on the organ, I consciously determined that I would experience the presence, being, and acts of God. Participating in the Communion meal of bread and wine was an excellent way to do this. When Communion ended I wondered how the church could celebrate the Lord's Supper more often. I felt that it was a significant part of worship.

Often I wish I could return to the attitude of worship I experienced as a boy. Particularly I think of attending evening worship at the East Pennsylvania Seventh-day Adventist camp meeting at Wescosville. Once my friend and I met the Voice of Prophecy vehicle as it entered the campgrounds. We ran alongside of it until it came to a stop at the guest facility. I had listened to their broadcast every Sunday morning. Besides singing along with the King's Heralds quartet, I had even tried to preach H.M.S. Richards' sermons when nobody was listening. Now I would hear them in person.

The large congregation became very quiet as the quartet sang gospel songs-some old and some new. The song just before Elder Richards spoke created a hunger in my heart to hear the Word of God. Elder Richards spoke conversationally about Jesus and His sacrifice for me. I loved his illustrations, but they never detracted from the word picture he was painting of God. The singers and the preacher never clouded my view of God. Like my robin friend, I wanted the refreshing to continue on and on.

Perhaps I appreciated most the spontaneity of camp meeting worship. A young man about 15 years old played a trumpet in quite a few meetings. His ability to triple-tongue his trumpet always amazed me. I tried to imagine what the gates to heaven looked like when he played "The Holy City." The expressions of amen rang through the large pavilion. I was always reticent to leave the meeting when it ended.

The fourth beatitude says: "Blessed are those who hunger and thirst for righteousness, for they shall be satisfied" (Matt. 5:6). When we acknowledge our spiritual poverty-open our hearts to God's forgiveness-we receive the peace that passes all human understanding. But that's not all. We receive a drive to worship in response to God's forgiving, reconciling, and renewing. Our quest to taste and see that the Lord is good becomes more intense until we are eager to celebrate God's presence, pardon, and peace. This overshadows what Peterson calls the singing, writing, witnessing, healing, teaching, painting, serving, helping, building, cleaning, and smiling. Rather, we find ourselves addicted to the main course of worship: God's presence, being, and actions.

Two attitudes endanger church and worship. The first is to abstain from worship because going to church and worshiping seem absurd in a world of atrocities and injustices. Many claim to stay away from church in a desire to provide time and energy to do something about the world predicament.

The second attitude is coming to worship to receive an adrenaline fix through entertainment. Congregational involvement is one antidote for this attitude. Such involvement across the generations will break any boredom.

Many times we dedicate the hour of worship to the business of the institutional church. When the hour is almost over and the congregants are tired and hungry, we then attempt to justify the gathering by a sermon interrupted by crying children and parents worried about the roast in the oven drying out beyond the ability of anyone to chew it.

If you are a good host, you offer your guests your undivided attention. You don't clean the house or repair the lawn mower. Instead, you listen to the stories and news that your guests bring and serve them a good meal. Forgiven sinners give full attention to the heavenly Guest. They listen, attend, and respond to His voice, focusing on bonding to their pardoning Savior.

The devil hates three important things: forgiveness, Sabbath, and the worship of the God of Creation.

Forgiveness speaks volumes about God's character. It forever squelches Satan's claim that the Lord is arbitrary and merciless. The devil works overtime to convince new Christians that they are not *really* forgiven, or he plants the idea that they have to do something to earn forgiveness.

Sabbath is a rehearsal for the great reunion when the Creator will bring all His faithful children together to enjoy eternal rest. It is a foretaste of the joy and praise we will experience when Jesus takes us to our eternal home. Satan tries to cancel out the blessedness of the Sabbath by tempting us to use the day for our own pursuits, or to fill the day with tight restrictions that keep us from delighting in Sabbath and the Lord of the Sabbath.

I attended a small Seventh-day Adventist academy my first time away from home. The mailman would drop the mail in a slot in the porch door where it would spill onto the floor. Very homesick, I'd look through the locked porch door and discover a letter from home, but the Sabbath rules at the school said that students could not receive mail on Sabbath. My Sabbath would have been much more delightful if I had been able to read the letter from the family who loved me. Some students managed to fish their letter through the crack at the bottom of the door using a wire with a hook on the end, but usually such attempts were unsuccessful.

The devil hates worship because it is an unmistakable sign of loyalty to our Lord and Savior. The last message to our dying world is an invitation to worship the Author of life. Satan wants us to be loyal to him so he can recruit as many as possible to join him in eternal destruction. The presentation of the last message about worship cannot be in word only. It must be demonstration as well as proclamation.

All three—forgiveness, Sabbath, and worship—are tied together securely by God's love. God invites us to enjoy all three. They can exhilarate people all around the world. We can rejoice in them as we meet in finely carpeted cathedrals or in simply furnished chapels.

I visited the beautiful country of Haiti two decades ago. The friendliness and the joy of the people particularly impressed me. High in the mountains I saw a church made of poles, purlins, and roof trusses covered with sheet metal. Its seating was nicely sawed planking. The pastor related to me how the members celebrated God's goodness every Sabbath. They came on foot from little villages surrounding the church, drawn by their gratitude to their Redeemer.

Eagerly I awaited the Sabbath so that I could hear and enjoy worship in a Haitian church. The people entered the church quietly and respectfully. Soon their voices filled the church with songs of praise. I could not speak their language, but I loudly hummed the melodies. I looked around me and noticed the bright smiles on the faces of the singing saints. The pastor preached in a language I could not understand, but I looked at the eager congregants turning the pages of their Bibles. Frequently they uttered expressions of approval and joy. Even though I could not understand what anyone said, I felt that I was standing at the very gates of heaven.

Soon I shall join my Haitian brothers and sisters along with those from every earthly land and island. Entering the heavenly world prepared for us, we will raise our voices together in thanksgiving for forgiveness and redemption. I don't know what language we will use, but one thing I do know. We will be excited about being in the presence of our Redeemer.

Chapter 9

FORGIVENESS
and the Fullness of Joy

Some time ago my wife gave me a mountain dulcimer kit for Christmas. I spent 50 hours constructing and finishing it. The booklet that came with the kit emphasized that there exists no one right way to play a dulcimer. So I placed it across my knees and began experimenting. In a few weeks I had mastered a few lively songs.

A few years later I noticed a professionally made dulcimer in a music shop. The owner invited me to play. The ring of the notes was so impressive that I bought it. Soon I was playing chords and learning various ways of strumming and picking. I felt pleased with my progress. Then it happened.

While driving through Hastings, Michigan, I noticed a dulcimer festival in progress. Unable to resist attending it, I went from booth to booth listening to people playing dulcimers. I bought tickets for a concert by the national dulcimer champion. As the master musician played his first selection, I could not believe that one musician could make that much music come from four strings.

"That fellow," I told my wife, "is compelling me to do one of two things—practice more or break my dulcimer in half." I sounded like a beginner next to him. What a humbling experience!

In an earlier chapter I mentioned the beatitude of acknowledgment—"Blessed are the poor in spirit, for theirs is the kingdom of heaven" (Matt. 5:3, NIV). Looking at the Master, studying His life, meditating on His character, jolts us from complacency and self-satisfaction. It is a humbling experience, reminding us of what spiritual paupers we are. The more we know about Him, the more we find ourselves forced to admit that we must change. We see ourselves as great sinners in need of a great Savior. Determination to be better doesn't work. Self-improvement leads only to more failure and discouragement. The only option is to acknowledge our true condition, confess our shortcoming, and open our life to His forgiveness and power.

The beatitude of the brokenhearted promises comfort to us when we mourn about falling short of God's purpose for us. Comfort comes as we allow the eternal streams of God's forgiveness to cleanse us from all unrighteousness.

As we realize that God gave all heaven in one Gift to redeem us from brokenness, we experience the calmness, gentleness, and meekness that the Holy Spirit brings into our life. Perhaps we can sum up the blessings in the beatitude of calm with one word-joy.

Joy is ours because we have discarded all inflated opinions of self. We have come to the realization that we have no spiritual superiority over others. Emptied of the last vestige of self, we have yielded to God's will. Above all, we sense relief, knowing that He has wiped the slate clean. With forgiveness come power and a desire to draw closer to Him each day.

The first three beatitudes are a recipe for self-emptying. This sets the stage for the beatitude of desire. "Blessed are those who hunger and thirst for righteousness, for they shall be satisfied" (Matt. 5:6).

Eugene Peterson colorfully paraphrased this passage. "You're blessed when you've worked up a good appetite for God. He's food and drink in the best meal you'll ever eat" (Message).

The empty calories of self-centered living never satisfy. God's forgiveness opens a totally new menu that now makes the former lifestyle-diet repulsive. The righteousness of Christ appears mouth-watering good. The born-again person craves God's soul-satisfying grace. Our appetite for God is His gift.

For 25 years I was a volunteer chaplain for hospices. Most of our patients were battling cancer. Their families prepared their favorite foods, hoping that they would provide strength to fight the disease. When mealtime arrived, though, the patients had no appetite. I have seen tears in the eyes of family members as they watched their loved ones seated listlessly in front of tasty meals. How sad it is when appetite has gone.

Sin robs us of our hunger for God. Parents have visited me about their children who have turned their back on God. Sorrow pierced their hearts as cold indifference and outright criticism met their appeals.

Thank God, He constantly taps the shoulders of the rebels. He uses ways to confront sinners with His love that we could never think of.

Archibald Rutledge tells of two men who had a severe argument in town. If others had not separated them, one of them would have been killed. After that night they both carried a gun, planning to end the argument for good. The one man, whom I shall call Ed, couldn't stand the suspense. He heard from Bill's field hand that Bill was planning to get him, so he decided to meet Bill halfway. He loaded his pistol and rode his horse the three miles to Bill's house. As he rode up the lane, he noticed someone coming toward him. It looked like Bill. Ed turned off the road into a large bay branch to hide. There he sat with his hand on his gun and the devil in his heart.

"I put up my left hand to pull aside a little limb," Ed said, "when on it I saw a white flower, a sweet bay flower. And I smelt it, too. My mother used to love that flower; and when I was a boy she made me bring a bush from the swamp and plant it in the yard for her. She was buried with one of them same white flowers in her hand. And, you know, I forgot all about why I had come down that road" (*Life's Extras* [New York: Fleming H. Revell Company, 1928], p. 18).

Bill approached the spot where Ed was hiding. Suddenly, Ed pulled out in front of him, calling to Bill as he did so. Something in the man's voice told Bill that it was safe. There in the middle of the roadway they settled their differences peacefully. All because of a little white flower.

Creating an appetite for His grace is God's specialty. The cancer of rebellion and sin is no match for God's magnetic love. His love can break the strongest chains of evil.

The fourth beatitude describes our desire for God as hunger and thirst. The two sensations imply that intense longings to partake of God's grace follow any true emptying.

Thirst was no stranger to me as I helped my father make hay on a hot summer day. After loading the wagon high with loose hay and emptying it into the haymow, we headed for the milk house. Usually I drank two big glasses of cold milk before going back for another load. I had thought I knew the extremes of thirst until I saw a photograph in Life magazine from World War II.

An American prisoner of war was reaching through a barbed-wire fence with a dirty cup in his hand. He stretched as far as he could. Just beyond his reach was a pipe flowing with fresh water. I gazed at that photograph for a long time, trying to put myself in that prisoner's place. I knew I had never thirsted to that extent.

My father and I once sat in a camp meeting pavilion, entranced as Keith Argraves recounted his experience as a prisoner during World War II. Starvation had reduced him and his fellow prisoners to mere skeletons. As he described the unceasing craving for food, I knew that my growing-boy hunger was a minor sensation compared to the hunger that Keith had felt.

The hunger and thirst that results from deliverance from sin are more than slight hunger twinges and mild dryness of the mouth. A compelling urge to partake of God's goodness and mercy takes possession of forgiven sinners. Every day they behold their spiritual poverty in contrast to God's riches. Every day they open to God's forgiveness and long for more of God's grace. And every day they find their longings satisfied.

The psalmists expressed this deep desire for God. "As the deer pants for the water brooks, so my soul pants for You, O God. My soul thirsts for God, for the living God" (Ps. 42:1). "My soul languishes for Your salvation; I wait for Your word" (Ps. 119:81).

The good news in the beatitude of desire is that God satisfies this hunger and thirst. Satisfaction became a reality for me while on a teaching itinerary in the Far East. After days of classes at a college in Indonesia, our gracious hosts took my wife and me on a tour of the countryside and visits to several church institutions. When we arrived at a mission office, cheerful women served us refreshments. An hour later our host took us to his home for more refreshments that turned out to be a full meal. Two hours later someone else invited us to a banquet in our honor. As we entered the banquet room I saw a large table covered with tantalizing food. That's when I longed for the hearty appetite of a teenager. Having eaten a short time before, I was able to take only small portions of the many foods. I reached a point at which I could not even make myself sample a few dishes that looked delicious. When the meal ended I felt satisfied beyond any time I had ever eaten before.

The joy of being filled and satisfied by the grace of God surpasses all the pleasures we could ever experience apart from God.

My wife hired a young teenager of the Amish faith to help her wash windows, blinds, and curtains. As they worked together the girl said, "I guess English [their term for non-Amish] kids think being Amish is boring." Quickly my wife told her that we had observed the youth of the Amish faith working and playing together. She complimented her and her faith for the family values that bring meaning to life. Then she told her that "English" kids may have more material things, but they do not bring meaning. Boredom easily sets in for them. We both assured our Amish friend that when you love God, life is not boring.

The beatitude of desire doesn't suggest that we hunger and thirst for joy and happiness. Rather, forgiveness brings hunger and thirst for more and more of God's grace. Thus joy and happiness are by-products of a satisfying relationship with God. Searching for joy is a sure way of having it elude us.

Joy is a solid conviction that no matter what happens, God will never leave nor forsake His own. It is deep gratitude for forgiveness and deliverance from besetting sin. And it is assurance of eternal life.

When I was a college student, a returned missionary spoke to the student body. He told us that he had buried his wife and two children in Africa, "but I am the happiest man in the world." I waited to hear his reason. The man told us that he knew God as his Savior and believed that there would soon be a great reunion. When Jesus returned, all sorrow and trouble would come to an end. He and his family would be together again. Although he spoke to us more than 50 years ago, his words still linger in my mind to encourage me when I need it.

John said: "God has given us eternal life, and this life is in His Son. He who has the Son has the life.... These things I have written to you who believe in the name of the Son of God, so that you may know that you have eternal life" (1 John 5:11–13). My missionary friend had the assurance of eternal life. That's why he could say, "I am the happiest man in the world."

Eugene Peterson paraphrased this passage: "My purpose in writing is simply this: that you who believe in God's Son will know beyond the shadow of a doubt that you have eternal life, the reality and not the illusion. And how bold and free we then become in his presence, freely asking according to his will, sure that he's listening. And if we're confident that he's listening, we know that what we've asked for is as good as ours" (verses 13–15, Message).

W. E. Vine's *Expository Dictionary of Biblical Words* states that "in the Old Testament and the New Testament God Himself is the ground and object of the believer's joy" (p. 336).

Joy is not based upon pleasant circumstances or good fortune, but on God and His faithfulness to us. We see this source of our joy as we examine a sampling of Scripture passages.

"In Your presence is fullness of joy" (Ps. 16:11).

"My soul shall rejoice in the Lord; it shall exult in His salvation" (Ps. 35:9).

"I will go to the altar of God, to God my exceeding joy" (Ps. 43:4).

"Wash me, and I shall be whiter than snow. Make me to hear joy and gladness.… Restore to me the joy of Your salvation" (Ps. 51:7–12).

After Jesus taught the disciples that continually abiding in Him is the only way to continually bear fruit, He said, "These things I have spoken to you so that My joy may be in you, and that your joy may be made full" (John 15:11). "Rejoice in the Lord always; again I will say, rejoice!" (Phil. 4:4).

Such passages show that joy is not dependent on transitory things. Its foundation is the assurance that God is our Friend and Savior, the same yesterday, today, and forever. The ancient people of faith maintained joy by resting securely in the salvation of the Lord. It opens us to the ministry of the Holy Spirit, who gives us the gift of joy (see Gal. 5:22).

A classic illustration of joy comes from the experience of the apostle Paul. He found God's forgiveness after planning the massacre of Christians. Thereafter he considered himself to be the chief of sinners. But he confidently preached forgiveness and joy.

Startling Paul out of sleep in Troas, a heavenly being invited him to preach the gospel in Macedonia. After all of that fanfare in the night he went to Macedonia, only to get thrown into a Roman dungeon. Imagine that! He sat in prison singing and praying until an earthquake shook open the prison. That is joy!

Dozens of people afflicted with a life-threatening illness have taught me how one can have joy even in the midst of adversity. One person particularly stands out in my mind.

Martha had suffered for months from incurable cancer. Her family called me to come to her bedside as her death approached. They were circling her bed when I arrived, most of them in tears. I squeezed into the circle by the head of the bed. I leaned down close to the woman's face and said, "What has been going through your mind today, Martha?"

She broke into a big smile as she told me what heaven will be like. Occasionally she managed a faint laugh as she put her imaginings into words. After almost 30 minutes she reached for my hand. With a faint smile on her face she said, "Pastor, I'm tired. I'll see you in the morning. It may be here tomorrow morning or it may be in the eternal morning."

My last words before prayer were "Martha, that's the blessed hope. We'll take a walk together in the morning."

Her daughter walked me to the door. "Pastor," she said, "I don't know much about what you and Mother were talking about. I never explored religion, but someday I want to have the joy I saw on Mother's face."

Martha had spent years hungering and thirsting for God. She had strongly bonded with Him because He had broken her bondage to sin when she was much younger. Thus she knew about heaven because she had learned to abide in Christ.

Bruce Wilkinson said: "Abiding is all about the most important friendship of your life. Abiding doesn't measure how much you know about your faith or your Bible. In abiding, you seek, long for, thirst for, wait for, see, know, love, hear, and respond to … a person. More abiding means more of God in your life, more of Him in your activities, thoughts, and desires" (*Secrets of the Vine* [Sisters, Oreg.: Multnomah Publishers, 2001], p. 103).

You can search for the meaning of prophetic trumpets, seals, thunders, and jubilees all your life without hungering and thirsting for God. And you can know the Book, even in the original languages, without knowing the One who inspired it. If all you have is book learning, you may not have Him and the joy that comes with His friendship.

Do you desire that joy? It can be yours by dropping the last vestige of self, receiving God's forgiveness, and hungering and thirsting for God. God delights in you. As you delight in Him, the Holy Spirit will impart lasting joy.

Chapter 10

FORGIVENESS—
Impact on Community

Children attending a summer camp in western Pennsylvania longed for their chance to swim in the lake. Crafts, hiking, and even meals seemed to be secondary to swimming. Two weeks into the camping season they began to complain about the smell of the water. They tried to avoid the swimming classes. The instructors who spent most of their time in the water complained that their skin itched and their eyes burned after a day in the lake.

The director of the waterfront walked around the lake, seeking a solution to the problem. Soon she noticed that the mountain stream that had filled the lake now flowed around it instead. The spillway was dry.

In an effort to warm the water for the comfort of the children, the camp director had asked the contractor who had built the lake to install a diverter and dig a channel around the lake. Before camp began he filled the lake, then sent the stream around it. No water flowed in or flowed out. The lake was warm, but stagnant.

The lake had to be made once again to fill with fresh mountain water and in turn spill the cool water back into the stream. Otherwise stagnation and foul smells kept the children from enjoyment.

The refreshing water of forgiveness flows continually from the heart of God. It fills the hearts of repentant sinners with peace, gratitude, goodness, and joy. The grace of God flows into the life, not only to bless the individual, but to water others who live a life parched by sin. As Ellen G. White put it, "Christ dwelling in the soul is a spring that never runs dry. Where He abides, there will be an overflowing of beneficence" (*Thoughts From the Mount of Blessing*, p. 22). Forgiveness cannot effectively carry out God's plan in the life of a self-centered person. If forgiveness cannot continue on to others, neither can it bring joy and peace to the individual. Stagnation and unpleasantness result.

John 7 records Jesus' visit to the Temple on the last day of the Feast of Tabernacles. The backdrop for His announcement that day was most impressive. The priests descended from Mount Moriah to the Pool of Siloam carrying empty pitchers that they filled with the cool water of Siloam. With full pitchers on their shoulders they returned up the slopes of Moriah. Every 10 steps they paused while the Levite choirs sang a song of praise for the river of life flowing to bless Israel. The slow procession continued through the Temple gates and ended in the courtyard.

The priests then took the water jars to the east of the altar where stood two lily-shaped basins made of gold. Into one basin they poured wine. Into the second they put the water. The liquids mingled together, flowed under the altar, and into the Kidron and on to the Dead Sea.

Against this backdrop Jesus stood up and cried with a loud voice, "If any one is thirsty, let him come to Me and drink. He who believes in Me, as the Scripture said, 'From his innermost being will flow rivers of living water' " (John 7:37, 38).

Once the grace of God fills His people, it overflows into the dry places of our sin-parched world. We receive forgiveness and reconciliation from God and in turn give it to others. Filling and spilling go hand in hand.

In the religious world we encounter much debate and controversy about worship styles, but seldom do we hear discussions about the goal of worship. Jesus set the example for us. He went into the presence of the Father, into the quiet place that included private prayer and synagogue worship. From there He ventured into the marketplace to bring blessings to others. He worshiped, then served—was filled, then spilled.

The religious leaders of Jesus' day resented His persistent outflowing of love to people on Sabbath and other days. Temple worship had become stagnant, but Jesus confronted the system that had clogged the flow of God's grace. He traveled day after day forgiving and healing. The leaders dogged His steps to find evidence in favor of His death.

Jesus intends for His body, the church, to be a community of the forgiven and a community of the forgiving all wrapped up in one. He desires the church to be both a community of the comforted and a community of the comforting. From the innermost being of the church must flow rivers of living water.

A church that gazes inward all the time will become stagnant like the lake in Pennsylvania. They will soon wallow in arguments about everything from plexiglass pulpits to rug colors. But a church that looks outward rejoices in the forgiving grace of Christ. And the larger society, seeing the difference, finds itself drawn to the community of the forgiven and forgiving.

American society living at the beginning of the twenty-first century presents some serious problems for the church. Robert D. Putnam, professor of public policy at Harvard University, shows by his research that during the last quarter of the twentieth century Americans had become more disengaged from one another. They did not join as many organizations and involved themselves less in community causes. The reduction of what he calls "social capital" is noticeable in every area of public life.

Giving to charity and volunteering have been and continue to be higher among churches than among secular community-based organizations. At the same time attendance and involvement in religious activities has fallen 25 to 50 percent in the past 25 years. And the more demanding the forms of involvement, the greater was the decline.

Putnam observes that "more and more Catholics are becoming merely nominal church members, while a large and steadily growing number of Protestants and Jews are abandoning their religion entirely.

Individually and congregationally, evangelicals are more likely to be involved in activities within their own religious community but are less likely to be involved in the broader community. The fundamentalist churches offer far stronger community to their members than do their moderate-liberal Protestant counterparts. The community-building efforts of the new denominations have been directed inward rather than outward, thus limiting their otherwise salutary effects on America' s stock of social capital. In short, as the twenty-first century opens, Americans are going to church less often than we did three or four decades ago, and the churches we go to are less engaged with the wider community" (*Bowling Alone* [New York: Simon and Schuster, 2000], pp. 72, 77, 79).

I saw this inwardness as I worked with the ministerial association in my community. Many of the more conservative pastors refused to attend our meetings even though we were simply trying to provide collegiality and time to share and pray together. Every year we produced a community Thanksgiving service and a community Good Friday service. The church board of the largest church in the community voted that their pastor could not participate, neither could anyone use their church sanctuary for any community services.

Such findings are alarming, especially when you think of Jesus' words: "You are the salt of the earth; but if the salt has become tasteless, how can it be made salty again? It is no longer good for anything except to be thrown out and trampled under foot by men. You are the light of the world. A city set on a hill cannot be hidden; nor does anyone light a lamp and put it under a basket, but on the lampstand, and it gives light to all who are in the house. Let your light shine before men in such a way that they may see your good works, and glorify your Father who is in heaven" (Matt. 5:13–16).

Instead of going into all the world with the gospel, many churches attempt to make the environment within the four walls of their church buildings exciting enough to draw people. Contemporizing worship services, installing coffee bars, opening fast-food restaurants, running fitness centers, providing free weight rooms, and featuring Christian rock bands will supposedly bring them in. Some observers feel that all of this smacks of further inwardness instead of genuine outreach to the world community.

Wade Clark Roof, professor of religion and society at the University of California, Santa Barbara, writes about the quest-culture created by baby boomers. He speaks about those who have become disillusioned with organized religion and now seek for whatever will provide deep meaning to life. He says that "the quest is for something more than doctrine, creed, or institution, although of course these are usually involved. What is sought after has to do more with feelings, with awareness of innermost realities, with intimations of the presence of the sacred—which amounts to the very pulse of lived religion. For if people do not encounter the sacred in profound, life-transforming ways through meditation, prayer, or other practices, the latter lose their force and risk becoming empty exercises" (*Spiritual Marketplace* [Princeton, N.J.: Princeton University Press, 1999], pp. 33, 34).

I believe that people on a spiritual quest are not going to be satisfied by the dazzle and sparkle of churches offering many of the world's amenities. They desire a church that takes the spiritual needs of the entire family into consideration. And they appreciate the opportunity of worshiping as a family, worship that incorporates people of all ages into the act of worship. I am impressed that the Beatitudes depict the experience for which the quest culture is searching.

The first three beatitudes describe what happens when we come into God's presence. The fourth assures us that He will satisfy our hunger and thirst for lived religion. Once we have our desire to partake of God's grace fully met, then we have more than a profession of faith. We spread out to the world to complete the mission begun by Jesus. The world sees that we have been with Jesus. The power of the Holy Spirit working through us will draw them to Christ. The very pulse of lived religion is more powerful than words alone.

We can more clearly understand the connection between

forgiveness and our relationship to the world community by examining the relationship between specific beatitudes. The first beatitude shows that the poor in spirit—the spiritual paupers—come into the presence of God, where they lose all pride and pretense. Their own inadequacies become clear, and they see themselves as they really are.

When they acknowledge their spiritual bankruptcy, they are able to show mercy to others as the fifth beatitude teaches. Instead of judging others, they encourage them. They do not meet them as superiors, but as friends who themselves have stumbled and fallen along the same pathway. Phyllis Tickle, contributing editor in religion for Publishers Weekly, views these qualities as vital to the very existence of the religious community and its ability to influence the larger community. "The religious community requires at least two things for survival: first, the absolute humility of every member before each other and before the God to whom all allegiance is owed; and second, the ability of every member to look out for every other member, lest any part stumble either spiritually or temporally and thereby threaten the worshiping and affianced whole" (*The Shaping of a Life* [New York: Doubleday, 2001], p. 258).

My son and I were hiking in British Columbia, ascending hilly rough terrain. I'm sure we appeared hot and tired to a group of hikers descending on the trail. Rugged, tanned, and well equipped for hiking, they could have chastised us for attempting the trail in sneakers, but they gave us words of encouragement. They spoke of the lovely views we would encounter along the way. As we parted we were much more positive about the trail ahead. I'm sure those experienced hikers knew of times when they also had tried to hike in sneakers.

The world is amazed when the poor in spirit show mercy and tolerance. Humanity may be puzzled by such kingdom behavior, but they will be impressed. They may even be surprised, because of having observed other religious people who did not deal with them in a compassionate manner. Tickle says: "Compassion is not a coveted spiritual virtue in the Christian religion. Christianity slices and dices virtues with all the same sense of nicety and exquisite seriousness as any other organized faith, of course; but it simply does not celebrate compassion's primacy among them in the life of grace" (Ibid., p. 268). It is tragic that this author had reason to make such a statement.

In the mid 1950s my wife and I attended an Easter sunrise service on the grounds of Walter Reed Hospital in Washington, D.C. The speaker was evangelist Billy Graham. He told about driving through a large Southern city. A car approaching an intersection on another street failed to yield the right-of-way. A loud crash sent people running to the scene of the accident. They noticed that one driver was White and the other was African-American. It heightened their anticipation of a fistfight.

Both drivers climbed out of their car and ran toward each other. Billy held out his hand and smiled at the African-American who also reached out his hand. Apologies flowed, and in moments the two men learned that they both were ministers of the gospel. They quietly exchanged insurance information and gave information to the police who arrived at the accident. The crowd looked on in disbelief and slowly left. Billy commented to his audience that the crowd could not believe what they had just witnessed. The poor in spirit are merciful.

The second beatitude teaches us that those who recognize and acknowledge their sin will then confess to God and open their lives to the flow of God's forgiveness. Self-centeredness vanishes and God imparts sincerity, honesty, and purity of motives. This imparted grace enables such individuals to treat others, as the sixth beatitude indicates, with honesty, sincerity, and pure motives. They are ready to offer forgiveness with or without apologies from those who offend them.

Such gracious treatment of others is possible because they have dropped their load of sin and guilt at the foot of Jesus' cross. He wants others to have the same experience. Ellen G. White says: "The Christian does not ask, Are they worthy? But, How can I benefit them? In the most wretched, the most debased, he sees souls whom Christ died to save and for whom God has given to His children the ministry of reconciliation" (*Thoughts From the Mount of Blessing*, p. 22).

Ellen G. White also pointed out that "nothing can justify an unforgiving spirit. He who is unmerciful toward others shows that he himself is not a partaker of God's pardoning grace. In God's forgiveness the heart of the erring one is drawn close to the great heart of Infinite Love. The tide of divine compassion flows into the sinner's soul, and from him to the souls of others. The tenderness and mercy that Christ has revealed in His own precious life will be seen in those who become sharers of His own grace" (*Christ's Object Lessons* [Washington, D.C.: Review and Herald Pub. Assn., 1900], p. 251).

One time I walked the floor of the Bay of Fundy at low tide. I looked up at the colossal rock formations that resembled giant flowerpots with vegetation on top. As the tide came in I headed for the steps that led to an observation platform overlooking the bay. The force of the tide rose higher and higher until nothing but the tops of those rock formations was visible. The water obliterated my footprints and the footprints of fellow tourists on the bottom of the bay. The tide covered our imprints in the sand, never to be seen again.

It stands to reason that when the tide of God's forgiveness erases your faulty footprints and you pass that forgiveness on to others, and God gives you power to begin again, you find peace, calm, and quiet assurance that you truly have eternal life. This experience naturally carries over to your relationship with the world around you. You become a peacemaker, as the seventh beatitude suggests. Not only do you bring peace to the world at large, you also bring peace into the community of faith.

As a very young pastor I looked up to a veteran pastor who was a peacemaker. When sharp differences of opinion about some theological point arose in pastors' meetings, he quietly listened to the heated debate. At the right moment he gently spoke words that were practical and gracious. He reminded us that the revelation of truth is an ongoing process that is not meant to divide, but to bring together. I happen to know that he was a peacemaker in his community also. Furthermore,

I understand that he made peace in his world because Jesus gave him peace in his own life.

Central to emptying, filling, and spilling over to the community is the fourth beatitude. All three depend on the Lord's ever-flowing stream of grace. Daily hungering and thirsting and daily satisfaction is the key to being a true witness, a convincing voice to the world community.

Jesus' death on the cross, His resurrection, and His daily ministry to us in the heavens make the community of the forgiven possible. The cross and the empty tomb are the heart of a people who continually abide in Christ and continually bear fruit in the world community. Jesus prayed for this in His intercessory prayer on our behalf found in John 17. He prayed for us because He knew that without our continually acknowledging our need, receiving His forgiveness, and finding satisfaction in the reinforcement of His grace, our witness to others would have no saltiness. In the world, but not of the world-that is the divine plan, but to carry it out successfully we must be in constant contact with the heavenly world.

Before leaving the Beatitudes, we must examine the word "blessed." Bruce Wilkinson said: "To bless in the biblical sense means to ask for or to impart supernatural favor. When we ask for God's blessing, we're not asking for more of what we could get for ourselves. We're crying out for the wonderful, unlimited goodness that only God has the power to know about or give to us" (*The Prayer of Jabez* [Sisters, Oreg.: Multnomah Publishers, 2000], p. 23).

I heard one speaker refer to blessings as many good things that are beyond human ability to produce. Isn't that what God wants for His people? Our eyes cannot see, nor can our ears hear, what God has in store for us. These blessings are bound to be a reality for us when we allow the forgiveness of God to flow through us to others.

Will we have difficulties as we continue to be conduits for God's grace? Yes, indeed. The eighth beatitude clearly states that we will experience persecution for righteousness' sake. When we participate in the work of salvation and restoration already in progress on God's part, we will face opposition. But as in the first seven beatitudes, the word blessed precedes the eighth beatitude. Even in the midst of opposition and difficulties, God's good things continue to flow.

A faithful Christian woman regularly brought her family of four children to church. Her husband fought with her every week about her faith, but she stood her ground. For years she felt alone and misunderstood by him. Then her blessings came in a mighty way when her children decided to live for Jesus and express that decision in baptism. Her face glowed with happiness when they entered the baptistry, yet she felt sorrow because her husband was not present to witness the event.

An evangelist came to town. Something about the advertising piece caught her husband's attention. At the same time the special meetings were held at the church he received a pink slip from the company he had worked at for 20 years. Now he had plenty of time to attend.

I was in their home when the big blessing came. Fred—I will call him that—was very quiet and thoughtful. Halfway through the visit he began to speak. "I want to tell my wife and my children that I am sorry for all the trouble I caused them. I argued and fought them about going to church for years, but I am not going to fight anymore. I have decided that I'm going to church with them from now on, and I am going to be baptized next Sabbath.".

I sat in a front pew and watched as Fred entered the baptistry. He never looked at the evangelist who baptized him. His eyes were riveted on his wife and children seated near the front of the church. A huge smile broke out, and love was written all over his face. Then I glanced at his wife and family. They wept and smiled at the same time. I have never seen such love dancing between people, not even during a wedding. Only one word could describe what I saw—blessings.

A few weeks later other blessings came to Fred. His company called him back to work, but he had to tell them he would not work on God's creation Sabbath. In spite of the fact that the company had never made any similar exception for anyone else, his employer granted him the privilege of observing Sabbath.

Living in the world community has plenty of dangers and pitfalls. We encounter obstacles that we cannot see our way around, over, or under. That's where the daily visitation of all the beatitudes enters the picture. Daily we empty self, then feast upon the grace of God on the mountaintop. There we look down upon the difficult obstacles. God gives us the insight and power to go down to the world community and successfully make our way through the problems.

Jesus did not pray that we would be in the world without providing the power necessary to maintain our faith. Daily communion with Him will open and close doors as necessary to keep us from falling. If we become discouraged, He will bring someone or something into our life to lift our spirits.

I worked in a hospital in which a teenage girl had both of her legs amputated after an accident crushed them. She was from a good Christian home, but her situation had caused her to despair of ever having happiness in life. The hospital personnel could not bring her out of depression. A nurse heard about another girl who was a double amputee. She had adjusted to the use of prostheses and was leading a meaningful life. Our staff invited her to be a "therapist" for our depressed patient.

In just a few days our "therapist" had the patient walking down the halls on her "stubbies," and eventually she learned to walk with full-size prostheses. We could hear the two of them chatting and laughing together. Life took on a totally different light because of the blessing God sent to her. Satan will do whatever he can to cripple us when we are walking with Jesus. He will send adversity, but Jesus is the therapist who will bless us in spite of the adversity. We have a mission to accomplish in the world community—a mission crucial to the completion of God's kingdom. You have His firm and unfailing promise—I will be with you, even to the end of the age.

Chapter 11

FORGIVENESS
and My Desire to Know God

Surgery was necessary if I was to continue working my way through school, but I knew that the cost could keep me out for years. At age 19 I made my way to the surgeon's office. He agreed that the operation should take place just before Thanksgiving vacation to reduce time away from classes.

Ten days after surgery the doctor entered my room, removed the bandages, and said to me, "Hey, kid, do you want to go home?"

"You better believe I do," I replied.

"Well, then, get dressed and get out of here," he ordered. In a moment he was out the door. A few seconds later he poked his head in the door. "How are you going to pay my bill, kid?"

"Don't worry, Doctor," I said. "I'll put in extra hours on the job and pay you as soon as I can."

"Go on home. You don't owe me anything." With that he was gone before I could utter a word of thanks.

A number of times I went by his home to say thanks, but he was never there. I managed to see his wife and asked her to pass my gratitude to her husband. That was 1952, but I am still curious about that surgeon. I have wanted ever since to know more about him.

Recently I met a retired surgeon in Arkansas. As we chatted I discovered that he had practiced medicine in the city where I had my surgery. In fact, I learned that he had privileges in the same hospital. I told him about my benefactor and noticed his eyes light up. "I know that man. He was on the hospital staff when I applied for privileges. Since I came from another country, the medical staff wanted to close the door on me, but the surgeon who operated on you was also my benefactor. He paved the way for my acceptance into the medical community. I shall always be indebted to him. Oh yes, I know him. He was an excellent surgeon and a true friend."

By now I am certain that my surgeon has died, but the desire to know him better has not diminished. My Arkansas friend gave me some insights, but I would be so happy to tell the man personally what his gift meant to me. It made the difference between staying in college or dropping out for a year or more.

This simple example of a human being extending a precious gift to me brings to mind God's great gift to the entire human race. The gift of forgiveness, like a reservoir of pure water, eternally flows to restore every person born into our world. While we were yet His enemies God sent His Son to take our sin upon His shoulders, then He placed His perfect life upon our shoulders. I don't know about you, but the thought of such a gift makes me desire to know Him better. His gift has opened the doors to new vistas that will expand from now until I walk into the kingdom of heaven. When I was attending school in Philadelphia I washed windows, mowed lawns, trimmed hedges, and served as a butler on weekends—anything to pay tuition, board, and room. I heard about an opening as an elevator operator in a nine-story apartment building behind the school. After applying and being accepted, I was excited until the boss, Mr. Vogt, told me that I would be expected to wear a suit and tie so as not to offend the wealthy people living in the apartment building. Thanking him, I told him I'd give him a final answer in a few hours.

Racing to the school, I told the principal, Robert Francis, my predicament. I had found a job but no clothes to fit the job. "Listen," Mr.

Francis said, "I may be able to help you. You look like you're about my size. I have a suit that I haven't worn for some time. The seat of the pants is a bit shiny, but you'll have your back to the wall of the elevator most of the time. The front of the suit looks quite nice. If you can fit into it, it is yours."

The suit fit perfectly. Returning to the apartment building, I told Mr. Vogt that I wanted to be his elevator operator. I think I was the only person aware of the shininess of the seat of the pants. Even Mr. Vogt thought I looked sharp. You and I have an invitation to live with God through out eternity, but we cannot go there in ragged clothes woven with the threads of our own making. We can't even get there with a shiny, worn suit. Instead, we must wear the robes of Jesus' perfect righteousness, the garments of holiness that cover our sinful self. I like to think that my robe is embroidered with the word "forgiven."

I do not understand most of the dynamics that go into that embroidered word, but I know who provided my robe. In my heart burns a desire to become better acquainted with Him. I cannot see Him physically, but I can see Him by faith as I read His Word and behold the miracles of grace that He performs in my life and that of others.

I have come to the realization that my embroidered robe is extremely expensive. I could never purchase such a garment, not even working many jobs the rest of my life. I have come to know that the only way to wear the robe is to accept it as a gift. A very expensive gift.

Also, I have come to see that I cannot wear the robe without paying the price of total self-surrender. Dietrich Bonhoeffer called it the high price of a free gift. Phyllis Tickle observed that "religion cheaply bought is cheaply valued" (*The Shaping of a Life*, p. 255).

When I value the gift I at the same time value the Giver of the gift. I have a growing urge to know Him better each day. To be in His presence is my constant desire.

Can you imagine how much Peter longed to know Jesus better after He forgave him for denying the Lord? Think of Nicodemus taking every opportunity to observe Christ after his "new birth" conversation in the night. Are you able to conceptualize the differ-ence in Bartimaeus' life after he was able to see? It wouldn't surprise me to learn that he went without three meals a day and even adequate sleep in order to accompany his Healer. Often I think that the woman forgiven so much spilled more than one bottle of precious ointment on Jesus' feet. I suspect that Zacchaeus turned the tables on Jesus by inviting Him back for dinner many times. How could he be satisfied with only one visit?

I was homesick the moment my parents dropped me off at the boarding school in Philadelphia. Slipping behind the school building, I waited until the tears dried and my eyes quit burning, then I entered the school to register for classes. As Jesus faded into the angel clouds the disciples gazed into the sky until they couldn't see Him anymore. Their eyes must have been full of tears. The angel assured them that their Benefactor would come just as He went, but their longing was to know more about Him. They had time to think about their faults. They opened themselves to forgiveness, and for the rest of their earthly journey they concentrated on knowing Him better.

Some people talk about getting to know God as though it is an extremely difficult undertaking. To the contrary, finding God isn't complicated.

My two grandsons were 3 and 6 when I played hide-and-seek with them. I hid my eyes and counted to 30 before announcing, "Coming, ready or not." Only a few seconds into my seeking I heard voices. From the 3-year-old I heard, "I'm in the closet!" The 6-year-old made funny noises. Both of them misunderstood. They didn't realize the object of the game was to hide so well that I couldn't find them. Actually, they loved the excitement of being found.

God is excited about being found. Alister E. McGrath wrote: "We are dealing with a God who reveals himself, who has taken the initia-tive away from us, who encounters us before we discover him. When we talk about 'revelation,' we are expressing the idea that God himself tells us who he is and what he is like" (*The Mystery of the Cross* [Grand

Rapids: Academe Books, 1988], p. 40).

"One of the most basic teachings of Christianity is that God chose to come to where we are. Instead of expecting us to find him, he comes to us. Some people think of religion as being like climbing up a ladder to find God. Yet Christianity affirms that God chose to come down the ladder to meet us, and then to bring us home rejoicing" (Alister E. McGrath, *The Unknown God* [Grand Rapids: Eerdmans Pub. Co., 1999], p. 58).

Where does God meet us most dramatically and convincingly? At the cross and the empty tomb. Jesus' disciples had their hopes shattered when the Roman soldiers stretched their Master on the cross, but resurrection turned it into a symbol of victory. The promise of return broadened their understanding of God's purpose. They gained a deeper understanding of His character. The cross and the empty tomb became the theme of their preaching and their daily conversation.

When you read the sermons of the apostle Peter you will hear him reviewing God's redemptive work that centers in the cross and the empty tomb. He writes about a living hope through the resurrection of Jesus Christ from the dead (1 Peter 1:3). The apostle tells about Jesus bearing our sins in His body on the cross (1 Peter 2 :24).

Read the writings of the apostle Paul and you'll meet a man who had tunnel vision that focused almost exclusively on the cross. To him the word of the cross is the power of God (Rom. 1:1–18).

John, the beloved disciple, gave us the favorite passage of John 3:16, which is bathed in the spirit of the cross.

The subjects of the cross and the empty tomb are inescapable for those who read the New Testament. They are the keys to forgiveness, redemption, and the final restoration of all creation. The messages of the cross and the empty tomb have tremendous power, not because they are neat theories or events, but because they represent God's action to deliver us from sin.

Alister E. McGrath wrote that "Christian faith is about an encounter with the living God, not about interesting ideas and concepts. The

Christian tradition, from the earliest times to the present day, has insisted that this encounter takes place through the cross and resurrection of Jesus Christ. Placed between us and the cross is a filter which it is necessary to remove—theories, hypotheses, and endless refinements of these, have been placed in the way of those who wish to return to the source and ground of the Christian faith. The Christian church must learn to return to where she once started from-the tension between the crucifixion and resurrection of Jesus Christ" (Ibid., p. 40).

The messages of the cross and the empty tomb reveal two things: The impotence of the human race and the extremes to which God has gone to restore His creation. When we stand in the light of the cross and the empty tomb, we see ourselves as we really are and receive a clear revelation of God's love and forgiveness.

"The more we study the divine character in the light of the cross, the more we see mercy, tenderness, and forgiveness blended with equity and justice, and the more clearly we discern the innumerable evidences of a love that is infinite and a tender pity surpassing a mother's yearning sympathy for her wayward child" (Ellen G. White, *Steps to Christ* [Washington, D.C.: Review and Herald Pub. Assn., 1908], p. 15).

Worship in the Christian community is an essential part of studying the divine character in the light of the cross. Group Bible study, delving into the great truths of the Scripture, uplifts and strengthens. We should not let philosophy and conjecture displace such study. The actual reading of Scripture is the heart of knowing God better.

I was invited to attend a Bible study group, but I refused to attend after a few sessions that seldom actually used the Bible. Expressions such as "the way I see it," "I think," "I can't see why," and "it would seem to me" dominated the entire session.

Cross-centered preaching and cross-centered singing and testifying comprise worship that acquaints us with God. Getting to know God in worship is characterized by the rustling of pages as the congregation uses their Bibles throughout the sermon.

Jesus did not leave getting to know God to chance. When He was nearing the close of His earthly ministry He promised to send the Holy Spirit to "teach you all things, and bring to your remembrance all that I said to you" (John 14:26).

Eugene Peterson paraphrased John 16:13: "When the Friend comes, the Spirit of the Truth, he will take you by the hand and guide you into all the truth there is" (Message).

The Holy Spirit is the ever-present teacher who clarifies truth and illuminates the character of God as we contemplate the cross and the empty tomb. The Teacher is available whenever we read God's Word and meditate on it.

When I was in the ninth grade I enrolled in algebra I from a correspondence school. All went well until I came to the lessons on quadratic equations. My work sheets came back from the distant instructor full of red marks. His explanatory remarks were brief, usually referring me to pages in the textbook. What I needed was a teacher who was physically present to explain quadratic equations. I am still unable to do quadratic equations.

The Holy Spirit illuminates our mind so that we can experience an ever-clearer understanding of the quadratic equations of salvation. The multidimensional nature of the cross and the empty tomb will unfold before us in an ever expanding manner, reaching throughout our life in eternity. The naïveté of those who write dogmatic opinions about the nature of Christ and the meaning of the cross always amuses me. Frankly, in this life we will probably never graduate from the elementary grades of redemptive studies. When we stand before the throne of God on the first day in heaven we will probably chuckle about our earthly degrees in theology. Our large tomes on theology will seem like *Dick and Jane* primers.

Knowing God better, despite the personal tutoring of the Holy Spirit, is a lifelong and eternal adventure. It all begins when the gift of forgiveness floods our barren souls and we gaze on the cross and the empty tomb that made it possible. The study of the cross and the empty tomb is similar in some ways to my recent experience with

10,378-foot Sandia Peak rising from the desert floor of New Mexico. At dusk I boarded the world's longest aerial tramway, 2.7 miles, to the peak. Shadows and shafts of fading sunlight created a strange mosaic of color. From the peak I saw the sparkling lights of Albuquerque.

As I watched from my motel the mountain changed with the angle of the sun. In early morning its blue and purple hues contrasted with the crisp blue sky. By the end of the day the warm glow of pinks and reddish-browns dominated the skyline.

Approaching the mountain from the northwest, I noticed a dark stormy sky behind the mountain. Rising somewhat mysteriously from the horizon, Sandia Peak wore many shades of pastel blue and gray.

The cross and the empty tomb provide me with fresh and often surprising glimpses of God. From the desert floor of sorrow, from the dizzying heights of joy, from the distant places of doubt, from the morning light of youth, and from the evening light of age, the cross and the empty tomb take on a meaning that meets my needs for assurance and peace. With a heart full of forgiveness I never tire of gazing at God's sacrifice for me. I can't learn enough about Him.

When World War II broke out I was about 9. My hero was a certain Army general who appeared in the newsreels shown at a local theater. I read stories about him in newspapers and listened to his speeches over the radio. Later I bought a long-playing record of his famous speech at West Point. I became angry when he was dismissed from his duty. The man could do no wrong—until I read biographies of his life and watched documentaries about him on television.

Reality tarnished my hero. The more I studied his life, the less I admired him.

Not so with Jesus. Our real Hero is the spotless Lamb of God, who has taken away the sins of the world. All the forces of evil warred against Him. Satan wanted desperately to bring about His fall, but He was victorious from infancy to the cross.

Since Satan couldn't defeat Jesus, he now feverishly attempts to cause us to fall, but the power of the cross and the empty tomb enables us to stand the test.

The apostle Peter said, "Humble yourselves under the mighty hand of Go.… After you have suffered for a little while, the God of all grace, who called you to His eternal glory in Christ, will Himself perfect, confirm, strengthen and establish you" (1 Peter 5:6–10).

Forgiveness creates a desire in the human heart to know God, but it is deeper than that. When God forgives us He endows us with the power of the Holy Spirit. We eagerly seek to please our Benefactor in a life of obedience, including harmonious relationships with others. These are the components of a growing friendship with Christ. Jesus, the friendship initiator, said, "This is my commandment, that you love one another, just as I have loved you. Greater love has no one than this, that one lay down his life for his friends. You are My friends if you do what I command you.

No longer do I call you slaves, for the slave does not know what his master is doing; but I have called you friends, for all things that I have heard from My Father I have made known to you. You did not choose Me but I chose you, and appointed you that you would go and bear fruit, and that your fruit would remain, so that whatever you ask of the Father in My name He may give to you" (John 15:12–16). Jesus is not talking about a casual friendship, but a deep intimacy that includes trust and transparency. Such friendship means feeling at home with Him.

Long after I married and left my parental home I continued to experience that at-home feeling. I felt free to explore the refrigerator at my parents' house when I was hungry. Keeping a steady stream of conversation flowing wasn't necessary. Stretching out in the porch hammock with a good book was a natural activity. My father, my sons, and I sat around the old cookstove in the evening eating Winesap apples and crackers pulled from the warmer above the cooking surface. None of us needed fancy china and silverware. My mother usually had a mixture of everyday tableware. The water glasses were jelly containers of many brands. That's the kind of at-home friendship Jesus has with us.

He doesn't force it. It is by invitation only. He said: "Behold, I stand at the door and knock; if anyone hears My voice and opens the door, I will come in to him and will dine with him, and he with Me" (Rev. 3:20). This is not the rushed lunch period. It is the evening meal after the day's work is done and you can relax with good food and fellowship. That's the friendship of Jesus.

Our friend Jesus will never abandon us. He told His disciples, "I will not leave you as orphans; I will come to you" (John 14:18).

Frequently I visited a woman in her late 50s. She was in the advanced stages of metastatic cancer, but it was not cancer that was breaking her heart. Her mother had died when she was a little girl. After the funeral her father dropped her off at the home of an aunt. He promised to come for her the following day.

After breakfast she sat in the bay window so she could see her daddy coming down the driveway. She sat there until the darkness obscured the road. When she fell asleep her aunt carried her to bed. The next day and the next she kept her vigil at the bay window, but her father didn't return. He never came. Now in her closing days of life she grieved for her father, who had never come back.

Not so with Jesus. He told us that He is preparing dwellings for us in heaven and will return at the appointed time to move us into the best real estate we have ever beheld. Yes, from our perspective there seems an apparent delay, but He will arrive on time.

During the waiting time we will encounter struggles, but our Friend will be there to steady our steps. "Do not fear, for I am with you; do not anxiously look about you, for I am your God. I will strengthen you, surely I will help you, surely I will uphold you with My righteous right hand" (Isa. 41:10). As Eugene Peterson paraphrased it: "Don't panic. I'm with you. There's no need to fear for I'm your God. I'll give you strength. I'll help you. I'll hold you steady, keep a firm grip on you" (Message).

When we become new Christians, new friends, we are connected to the Vine. We are new branches in Christ. Although we may be too young in the faith to be fruitful, Jesus, the vinedresser, knows how to mature us to make us fruitful.

Jesus said that "every branch *in Me* that does not bear fruit, He takes away" (John 15:2). Bruce Wilkinson observes that the fact that we are *in Christ* determines how we render the phrase "take away." He states that the word can be translated "take up" or "lift up."

A California vineyard owner told Bruce that young branches often trail down and grow along the ground. There they gather dust, mud, and mildew that keep them from bearing fruit. The vinedresser lifts the young vines, cleans them, and ties them to the trellis where they can thrive and bear fruit (*Secrets of the Vine*).

Our friend Jesus, like the vinedresser in California, does everything necessary to make our relationship with Him fruitful. Along with careful tending He gives us joy and full assurance that no matter what difficulties arise, He is still in control, still the guardian of our soul.

My friend Alfred married a gracious woman after both of them had lost a spouse to cancer. Shortly after their third anniversary Alfred received the diagnosis of a fast-moving cancer. In his weakened condition he felt that he couldn't do anything to make Ann happy. I told him, "Alfred, God is still in control of your life. You can pray, 'God, I empty my hands of all vestiges of self. I come to You with empty hands to receive some gift for my wife.'"

I told him the gift might be things as simple as a thank you, a smile, or a good-morning. "Each day," I told him, "you can come to Jesus with outstretched hands to receive a gift for Ann. You can have joyous days with Ann even though you are sick and weak."

Two days later I sat in Ann's living room listening to her story. "Alfred was so happy about praying with open hands. Yesterday morning I came to his bedside as he was dying. He was too weak to speak, but as he was dying he held his open hands out to God."

Alfred's heavenly Friend truly kept His promise. "These things I have spoken to you, so that My joy may be in you, and that your joy may be made full" (John 15:11).

Thus Alfred had no reason to be afraid of death because his friend

Jesus promised to resurrect him on the last day of earth's history.

Jesus promised: "This is the will of Him who sent Me, that of all that He has given Me I lose nothing, but raise it up on the last day. For this is the will of My Father, that everyone who beholds the Son and believes in Him will have eternal life, and I Myself will raise him up on the last day" (John 6:39, 40).

Forgiven sinners walk with their friend Jesus from the infancy of their born-again experience to the very end of their earthly journey, only to meet their friend again at the resurrection.

Parts of our journey may leave us weary, but traveling with our friend Jesus renews our courage to continue. He invites us to "come to Me, all who are weary and heavy-laden, and I will give you rest. Take my yoke upon you and learn from Me, for I am gentle and humble in heart, and you will find rest for your souls. For My yoke is easy and My burden is light" (Matt. 11:28–30).

One morning in the Philippine Islands I passed a peasant farmer on my way to an appointment. He was plowing with a water buffalo. At the end of every furrow he stopped to rest his buffalo and himself. At noon I passed by the field and saw the farmer bathing the buffalo's shoulders. The yoke was propped against a tree. After the bath the buffalo sprawled under the tree and the farmer lay down next to the animal for a nap.

Later I spoke to a man who lived in the Philippines. He told me that the water buffalo was a farmer's prize possession. Any wise farmer knew that without the animal he faced starvation, therefore he put the buffalo's comfort ahead of his own.

How much like the Friend of the forgiven sinner. He bore our sins on His shoulders so that we might have rest and a light load.

Chapter 12

FORGIVENESS—
Two-in-One Package

Boys attending a summer camp in Ohio excitedly gathered by the flagpole in preparation for an evening hike over rugged hills. Our destination was a clearing two miles from camp where we would sleep under the stars. Each boy would carry his own bedroll and a flashlight. I threw my bedroll in the chuck wagon parked by the campsite. I figured that a counselor should have a perk now and then.

Ten minutes into the hike boys began groaning under the weight of their bedrolls. Their pace slowed, and some simply plopped down and refused to budge. I behaved like an Army drill sergeant. "Get up and move! Be a man! That roll isn't that heavy!" I yelled. But my orders fell on deaf ears. Since I was assigned to bring up the rear, I knew I had to find a solution. One by one I piled bedrolls on my shoulders and convinced the now-lighter slowpokes to stumble forward, but something began happening to me as I added bedroll after bedroll to my shoulders. My Army sergeant demeanor disappeared. My voice became gentle and more encouraging. The load on my shoulders produced sensitivity and tenderness toward the little dropouts along the trail. A transformation happened when I felt aching muscles and experienced exhaustion myself.

Sinners who behold the beauty and perfect righteousness of Jesus find themselves convicted of their own lostness, lastness, and leastness. They open to the streams of forgiveness and power. The calm of the Holy

Spirit fills their lives, and they hunger and thirst for life-transforming grace. And they never forget the heavy load of sin that brought despair and fatigue. The inclination to judge others disappears. Reacting mercifully to those who struggle with sin, they have a forgiving attitude toward all who cause them personal pain and loss. Because they know what it was like when they themselves carried a heavy load, they can readily forgive. The grace that fills them now spills over to fellow travelers on the journey of life.

Dying daily to self and being raised to new and invigorating spiritual life—following the path of the cross and the empty tomb—is the secret to maintaining an attitude of forgiveness toward all who trespass against us. And it is the key to reconciling with those we have offended.

God's power operating in the life of His children produces restoration and renewal in all human relationships. When the other party is not receptive to renewal or refuses to communicate, God enables a person to forgive unilaterally. The power to forgive does not arise naturally within us. The infusion of the Holy Spirit's strength transforms us in the light of the cross and the empty tomb, producing peacefulness and forgiveness toward others.

Annette is a good example. She refused to have an abortion when she was expecting her son. Pressure from her husband and his family put her through merciless emotional torture, but her faith in God helped her to endure it. After the baby's birth, her husband stayed away from home and eventually divorced her. He took their son with him. When Annette learned where her son was staying, her husband relocated him. But she could not afford legal assistance to gain contact with him. She told me that she "held a grudge and was angry all the time." So I prayed for help each time I started to feel resentment. I prayed for help to be forgiving. God softens my heart and gives me peace over the situation. My only help is God and Him helping me to love and forgive those who are hurting me and my son. I rest my case in God's hands and know He will make all things beautiful in His time."

For Annette, forgiveness is not an innate quality. Realizing that it is a gift from God, she repeatedly asks for it and repeatedly thanks God for helping her to forgive.

Dave Pelzer is another example of Spirit-infused forgivingness. His drunken and drugged mother never called him by his name. She beat him severely and separated him from the family for long periods of time. Many times he thought he would die from the inhumane treatment, but he always prayed that he could live long enough to make something of himself. He desperately wanted to please his mother and prove that he was a worthwhile person. Finally he married and left home. Dave dearly loved his little son, Stephen.

"Stopping in front of me, Stephen asked, 'Do you forgive her? I mean, your mom?' Kneeling down, I held him by his shoulders. 'Absolutely'" (*A Man Named Dave* [Plume, N.Y.: 2000], p. 259). Dave went on to make allowances for his mother, who never had anyone to whom she could tell her troubles. He told Stephen not to hate anyone and not to go to bed upset, but to talk about situations rather than allowing them to simmer. Above all, he stressed to his son that hate will eat away at you and will waste your life.

Dave Pelzer's forgiveness of his mother also was not innate. God answered his hundreds of prayers for the strength to love and forgive. He was exercising the gift of forgiveness that the Lord gave him for his mother.

Colleen Townsend Evans wrote that "forgiveness can work only if it flows from God to us and on to others. If we hold it to ourselves, refusing to pass it on, we destroy it. Until we ourselves have been forgiven by God, we cannot truly forgive others, but once we have accepted his divine pardon, we cannot refuse to give it away to others" (*Start Loving—The Miracle of Forgiving* [Garden City, N.Y.: Doubleday and Company, 1976], p. 76).

The reason we cannot refuse to give it away is that forgiveness transforms us. Now possessing the mind of Christ, we become unobstructed vessels through whom God can bring His healing grace to the world.

The drainage pipe that carries water away from the foundation of my house was not performing well. When I dug the ground away from the end of the pipe I discovered that a bulldozer used to grade the lawn had flattened the last 15 feet of the pipe. The blockage caused a buildup of sediment in the remainder of the pipe. I removed the flattened pipe and cleaned the undamaged pipe with a high-pressure water hose, allowing the water to flow freely.

God's forgiveness removes the things that keep His grace from flowing to us and through us. It purges the accumulation of damaging habits and negative attitudes from our hearts, removing self-centeredness, thus allowing God's love to permeate the heart. In turn, that love spreads to others.

Why is God so intent on transforming us into open vessels? Why is forgiveness and forgivingness wrapped in the same package?

Because forgiveness is the avenue into His kingdom. Forgiveness and forgivingness accompany each other because we are living reminders of Jesus to the world. We are participants in His ministry. Jesus came to save all people from their sins, and we are God's instruments for demonstrating and proclaiming that forgiveness and forgivingness. Jesus is the forgiver who shattered the ecclesiastical world of His day. Religious leaders had become pious police officers ready to chastise others at the least infraction of the rules. As a result, people found attendance at religious services threatening and unpleasant. Jesus roamed the streets and villages, attended synagogues, and visited individuals in their homes. He perfumed every place He went with the aroma of love, forgiveness, and the power to live joyfully.

The Holy Spirit motivates and empowers forgiven sinners to do exactly the same thing. Jesus was a living reminder of God, and we are living reminders of Jesus, carrying out the mission that He began.

We successfully reveal Jesus the forgiver to others when we spend much time with Him. In our discussion of the Beatitudes we mentioned that they describe a daily acknowledgment of our sinfulness, a daily emptying of self-centeredness and pride from our hearts, and a daily opening to God's refreshing stream of forgiveness. Daily we bask in God's presence and power. Beholding His character changes us into His likeness. Thus we remind the world of Jesus by loving, giving, and forgiving as He does.

I am convinced that forgiveness toward others does not have its genesis in the human heart. Henri J. M. Nouwen wrote: "Indeed, something has to happen that I myself cannot cause to happen. I cannot be reborn from below; that is, with my own strength, with my own mind, with my own psychological insights. I can only be healed from above, from where God reaches down. What is impossible for me is possible for God. With God everything is possible" (*The Return of the Prodigal Son*, p. 76).

Desmond Tutu's account of the work of the Truth and Reconciliation Commission in South Africa tells of dozens of cases in which victims forgave the perpetrators of crimes against them. One, Neville Clarence, lost his eyesight as a result of a car bomb explosion. He attended the amnesty hearing and faced a Mr. Ismail, one of those who had carried out the deed. "I have absolutely no grudge whatsoever to bear, never have and never will," he stated, "against the perpetrators of that car bomb explosion" (*No Future Without Forgiveness*, p. 154). Clarence shook hands with Ismail and expressed his forgiveness. It was as if they didn't want to let go of each other as they shook hands, he said. The picture of the two shaking hands, splashed across newspapers and TV screens, offered a testimony of the God-given gift of forgiveness.

I maintain that God's forgiveness alone transforms, motivates, and enables us to forgive others. We do not go through a series of psychological steps carefully outlined in self-help books. When the Holy Spirit accompanies the gift of forgiveness, forgiving others is an integral part of that divine act.

Many authors and preachers see conditionality in the part of the Lord's Prayer that says, "And forgive us our debts, as we also have forgiven our debtors" (Matt. 6:12). I see this as a prayer for both forgiveness and forgivingness because you can't have one without the other. They come in the same package.

Ellen G. White wrote: "We are not forgiven *because* we forgive, but as we forgive. The ground of all forgiveness is found in the unmerited love of God, but by our attitude toward others we show whether we have made that love our own" (*Christ's Object Lessons*, p. 251).

When we make God's love our own, it floods our life with forgivingness. It is unthinkable that our life could be filled with God's graces without the desire and ability to forgive others.

Ellen G. White emphasized this when she wrote, "Nothing can justify an unforgiving spirit. He who is unmerciful toward others shows that he himself is not a partaker of God's pardoning grace. In God's forgiveness the heart of the erring one is drawn close to the great heart of Infinite Love. The tide of divine compassion flows into the sinner's soul, and from him to the souls of others. The tenderness and mercy that Christ has revealed in His own precious life will be seen in those who become sharers of His own grace" (Ibid.).

Jesus told a parable about a man forgiven a huge debt owed to a rich king (Matt. 18:21–35). Shortly thereafter he grabbed by the neck a fellow who owed him a small amount. In spite of the debtor's plea for mercy, he threw him into jail.

This parable emphasizes that the reception of God's forgiveness must always include the willingness and strength to forgive others. Closer examination of the fine points of the parable shows that the man didn't acknowledge the enormity of his debt or his inability to pay it. Instead, he told the king that he could pay, given some time. He certainly didn't display the poor-in-spirit attitude.

A cursory reading of the parable causes some to teach that God withdraws His forgiveness. Ellen G. White discounts this idea. "It is true that he may once have received forgiveness; but his unmerciful spirit shows that he now rejects God's pardoning love. He has separated himself from God, and is in the same condition as before he was forgiven. He has denied his repentance, and his sins are upon him as if he had not repented" (Ibid.,.

Interesting as these thoughts may be, the key lesson of the parable remains. Forgiveness and forgivingness come wrapped in the same package.

Benefits of the Two-in-One Package

Credibility

The body of Christ, the church, has received a commission from Jesus. That commission compels us to spread the good news of eternal life to the entire earth. At its heart is the exciting announcement that Jesus came to save us from our sin. The cross and the empty tomb make forgiveness, reconciliation, and new life in Christ a reality. We are telling the world that God's forgiveness flows to everyone and that opening the life to that forgiveness brings assurance of eternal life. God's forgiveness with its accompanying ability to forgive others creates a community that is credible. The church is like a theater that dramatizes forgiveness for all to see.

The authorities had Peter and John arrested and brought before them for proclaiming the resurrection of Jesus. The rulers asked the two men by what power they spoke and healed. Peter responded by focusing on the resurrected and forgiving Christ as the source of healing and eternal life.

His words stunned the rulers. "As they observed the confidence of Peter and John, and understood that they were uneducated and untrained men, they were amazed, and began to recognize them as having been with Jesus" (Acts 4:13). Their message and their life corresponded. They were credible.

The apostolic church blossomed and bore much fruit because they had put aside differences and divisions. Its members spoke with authority because their lives demonstrated their unity. This was an answer to Jesus' prayer for us in John 17. He asked the Father to make us one, perfected in unity, so that the world may know Him. It is still an effectual prayer that will make the community of the forgiven and the forgiving a witness difficult to dispute.

Freedom to Grow

Holding grudges and harboring resentment are like prison bars that keep you from basking in sunlight and breathing in fresh air on a mountaintop. When you experience God's forgiveness, the bars of bitterness melt away. You are free to take in God's grace, which promotes spiritual growth.

A pastor told me about forgiving an aunt who had become a "thorn in my flesh." For years the resentment simmered, but one day he asked her to forgive him for his ill feelings toward her. She graciously forgave him. "I felt a heavy load slip off my shoulders," he told me.

When visiting another country I noticed quite a few stooped older women. Nationals explained that when they were young girls the women had carried their younger siblings on their backs as they bent over to plant rice. Long days of such labor rendered them permanently stooped. Today modern ways have changed the custom. Young women stand erect and appear in good health.

Forgiveness and forgivingness lift heavy loads. We can stand erect and walk in the paths of righteousness.

Good Health

Holding grudges usually involves anger that may even develop into a habit caused by many years of rehearsing personal injuries and injustices. Numerous authorities associate such anger with health problems. Gerald G. Jampolsky, M.D., wrote: "As a physician for more than forty years, I can recall people with a variety of illnesses-from back problems, to ulcers, to high blood pressure, and even to cancer-who have had many of their symptoms abate as they learned to forgive. I have been heartened in recent years to see research emerging that shows a relationship between forgiveness and health. We now know that lack of forgiveness-that is, clinging to anger, fear, and pain-does have a measurable impact on our bodies. These create tensions which affect the physiological systems that we are dependent on for health. They affect the circulation of blood in our bodies. They affect the efficiency of our immune systems. They put stress on our hearts, on our brains, and on virtually every organ in our bodies. Lack of forgiveness is indeed a health factor" (*Forgiveness: The Greatest Healer of All* [Hillsboro, Oreg.: Beyond Words Publishing, 1999], pp. xxiv, xxv).

"Research into the psychophysiology of human stress has shown us that the thoughts and feelings we hold in our minds are frequently translated into physical symptoms or emotional disorders: anxiety, depression, agitation, poor self-esteem, headaches, backaches, pains in the neck, stomachaches, and compromised immunity that can make us prone to infection and allergies. Our own judgments and unforgiving thoughts can also be translated into stress responses that literally attack our own bodies" (Ibid., p. 57).

No wonder my pastor friend said he felt a heavy load slip off his shoulders after he forgave his aunt. He may have intended it as a figure of speech, but he may well also have opened the way for better health.

Happier Family Life

The chief of psychiatry at the hospital where I served as chaplain once told me, "Chaplain, I have one of those impossible cases for you. A marriage is coming apart. Religious differences seem to be involved, but I'm not into that religion stuff. Maybe you can help. You seem to like to deal with incurables."

The husband belonged to a very demanding religion. He was trying to comply with all the little requirements and suggestions of his religious advisers, but he didn't stop to think how his involvement in nonessentials was separating him from his wife. Frightened because he insisted on taking the children to a religious celebration halfway across the continent, she had visions of her children being poisoned in a Jonestown-like incident. But she could not verbalize her fears, and his stubborn attitude eroded all tenderness and intimacy from their marriage. Both of them were deeply hurt, and trust was rapidly slipping away from the relationship.

When I met with them we spent a lot of time discussing Jesus' life and His mission to save us from our sin. We looked at His ability to understand people and His unconditional forgiveness. Both of them agreed to spend time meditating on Jesus' character. I suggested that they pray together even though they had different religious affiliations.

The turning point came nearly two months after they began visiting with me. The wife turned to her husband and expressed her love for him. She spoke of her hopes and dreams for their home. At last she was able to talk about her 'fears, and he listened. I looked at him and noticed that tears were streaming down his face. When she finished she was sobbing and he was holding her close. Assuring her that he did not mean to hurt her, he agreed that he had gone overboard in his religious life. He admitted to her that God did not want him to hurt her and their home. Then he apologized profusely, and she accepted his apology with a tight embrace.

A year later I received a letter from them. They thanked me for taking time with them, and they expressed gratitude to God for putting their marriage back together.

I have seen bitterness and an unforgiving spirit rip homes and marriages apart. I have seen children move out of their parental homes because forgiveness and forgivingness were absent. On the other hand, I have seen marriages and homes on the brink of destruction rebuilt by a new relationship with God, forgiveness, and the free exercise of forgivingness.

In some cases marriages dissolve and one of the partners refuses to communicate, scorning all efforts to resolve differences. But unilateral forgiveness brings peace to the party who wants to make things right even though he or she does not receive an opportunity to do so. A woman divorced her husband because of serious abuse. Her children bitterly urged her never to forgive him, but she had a relationship with Jesus. Forgiveness was a well-developed pattern in her life. She told her children that she forgave so that she could be a better mother and a whole person. Forgiveness healed her broken heart and enhanced her relationship with others.

A man who attended a bereavement support program that I conducted told the group his secret of a happy marriage. He said that every evening he and his wife reviewed the events of the day. They apologized for any hurt they had caused. Then they prayed together and sincerely spoke the words "I love you." Their marriage was rewarding and healthy because of forgiveness and forgivingness.

Wider Community

America is a lonely place to live because high technology and increased mobility have separated people instead of bringing them together. Housing developments are mushrooming and crowding out farmers, but the high-end houses diminish chances of creating close community.

Families leave early for work and close their garage doors behind them when they return. They settle down to watch a DVD—out of sight for the evening.

James J. Lynch wrote that "dialogue is the elixir of life and chronic loneliness is lethal poison. Based on recent health trends, it is growing ever more apparent that New Age cultural forces that disturb, disrupt, and destroy human dialogue must be viewed with the same concern and alarm as has been brought to bear on other plagues, infectious diseases, viruses, bacteria, and cancers. For all of the recent health data suggest that if current trends persist, *communicative disease,* and its resultant loneliness, will equal *communicable disease* as a leading cause of premature death in all post-industrialized nations during the twenty-first century" (*A Cry Unheard* [Baltimore: Bancroft Press, 2000], p. 1).

Anger, resentment, and unforgivingness cause some to experience communicative isolation, exile, and loneliness. In addition to putting stress on the heart, such things shrink their community and their chances at experiencing the many kinds of intimacy essential for a full life. The unforgiven heart is an unforgiving heart that turns others away. When God's grace fills the heart, though, it draws people to us because we are now genuinely interested in them. We become uplifting and encouraging company.

Allowing God's grace to flow through us to others can be exciting and rewarding. Even though I am reserved by nature, I have learned to reach out to people I meet-and I intentionally go out of my way to meet them. Clerks, servers in restaurants, occupants of park benches, people waiting for flights, and even long-distance telephone operators can enlarge my community. I've made friends in the "men's department" of Wal-Mart. (That's the benches where men wait for their wives to finish shopping.) I go to auctions at which I'm always amazed at the amount of personal information people share with me as we paw through the odds and ends for sale. I see many of the same people at each auction, so it is a kind of reunion.

In the process I have discovered that being at peace with God helps me to carry peace into the world around me. That is precisely what Jesus did. He would go to a quiet place where He held deep communion with the Father, then return to the villages and byways to spend Himself for others.

Improved Prayer Life

You may have noticed that when you see a person who has offended you, you avoid them if you have not extended forgiveness to them. Lack of forgiveness and forgivingness can actually close all communication. It is certainly true of our talking with God.

On the other hand, when all is well with God and human relationships, prayer is much more than the habitual "God is great, God is good" carried over from childhood.

For the forgiven sinner prayer is an experience of transparency that hides nothing from God. We don't have to carefully calculate what to say or make our words flowery. As Ellen G. White put it, "prayer is the opening of the heart to God as to a friend." It is relaxed and unrehearsed. You know you have spoken to One who has listened to you.

Forgiven sinners, emptied of the last vestige of self, open their hands to others. Then God fills the empty hands with blessings that they promptly empty into the hearts, homes, churches, and communities nearby.

The late Henri J. M. Nouwen emphasized that the prayer life of a forgiven sinner is not limited to a few moments before a meal or a quickie before crawling into bed. To pray is to live. Praying is discovering yourself, your God, and your neighbor.

Forgiveness and forgivingness is the heavenly two-in-one package that not only brightens the world we live in now. Throughout eternity we will celebrate the gift and study the Redeemer who made the gift possible.

Chapter 13

HEAVEN—
A Celebration of Forgiveness

My father and I drove to Womelsdorf, Pennsylvania, in his much-used 1935 Ford. After purchasing a few milk cows, he coasted the Ford down the incline behind the cattle dealer's barn. He slipped the car into second gear and released the clutch to start the motor. It was the World War II era, when batteries were rationed and scarce. Using the starter would have put a strain on the battery and shortened its life.

As we neared the city of Lebanon traffic became heavier and slower. Once we reached the city limits the cars barely moved and their drivers blew their horns. People were dancing on the sidewalks, jumping up and down on car roofs, throwing paper out of upper-story windows. My father rolled down his window and asked a man what all the excitement was about. "Don't you know, mister? The war is over!" he yelled.

My rather conservative father turned to me and said, "Battery or no battery—I'm going to blow the horn!" He honked it until we reached Cornwall Pike leading to home. After years of watching little star banners appear in home windows, each one signifying a son killed in action, we were ready for peace. We had seen too many trainloads of new tanks and jeeps passing through our quiet farmlands. The sounds of weeping and praying for soldier boys from our church had gone on too long. Planes from a nearby air base practiced peeling off maneuvers and dogfighting above our farm. While it fascinated my boyhood love of adventure, I also knew that it meant tragedy and death in Europe and the Pacific. My brother and my uncle Ray were in the military. I had spent too many nights wondering if they were still alive.

We were ready to celebrate, and celebrate we did.

Every one of us has been in a long spiritual battle. The enemy of souls, Satan, has waged war for many centuries. He has exposed humanity to genocide, ethnic cleansing, child and spouse abuse, pornography, murder, divorce, civil war, and worldwide conflict. The devil has even invaded the church in an effort to weaken its witness. No segment of society has escaped his evil attacks. God's children are ready for peace. We are ready to celebrate the end result of forgiveness and forgivingness. Each one of us longs to celebrate eternal freedom from everything that destroys life as God meant it to be in the beginning. And celebrate we will.

The celebration of forgiveness, however, cannot wait for the second advent of Christ and our entrance into the dwelling places Jesus is preparing for us. The wayward son in the story of the prodigal father was rushed to a celebration dinner as soon as he had a chance to bathe and the servants were able to cook the fatted calf. The son had been freed from the shame of rebellion and poverty. The father celebrated the son's reclamation, but the son celebrated his forgiveness. From all appearances, the celebration occurred the same day the son returned.

Back in the days of the psalmists God's followers were celebrating forgiveness and other aspects of His goodness. A quick look at Psalms 145 to 150 will show this. "The Lord is gracious and merciful; slow to anger and great in lovingkindness. The Lord is good to all, and His mercies are over all His works. All Your works shall give thanks to You, O Lord" (Ps. 145:8 10). "The Lord is near to all who call upon Him, to all who call upon Him in truth. He will fulfill the desire of those who fear Him; He will also hear their cry and will save them" (verses 18, 19). "He heals the brokenhearted, and binds up their wounds" (Ps. 147:3).

"He will beautify the afflicted ones with salvation" (Ps. 149:4).

Their celebration is not raucous, but emotionally stirring. In addition to singing, we find them playing upon trumpets, harps, lyres, timbrels, stringed instruments, pipes, and cymbals. I haven't any idea what dancing in their worship was like, but it is clear that these people put their whole being into worshiping God. It was a genuine celebration, not an hour of lecturing. They participated in the enjoyment of God's goodness.

Once I attended a concert given by the National Symphony Orchestra and a huge choir of more than 200 singers in a performance of G. F. Handel's oratorio *Messiah*. I was literally on the edge of my seat as they sang the words of Revelation 5:12, 13: "Worthy is the Lamb that was slain, and hath redeemed us to God by His blood, to receive power, and riches, and wisdom, and strength, and honor, and glory, and blessing. Blessing and honor, glory and power be unto Him that sitteth upon the throne, and unto the Lamb forever and ever. Amen."

As they approached the finale of the Amen Chorus, the singers increased their volume. The sopranos soared effortlessly to high A. The tenors followed them. Every brass player held instruments high so their notes would ring with crescendo force. The strings and woodwinds supported the shrill call of the trumpets. The timpanist relentlessly beat his kettledrums with mallets that became virtually invisible. With uplifted arms the conductor begged the orchestra and choir to give their best to the final chord, then brought the music to a close with a vigorous downbeat.

Instantly a man in the audience leaped to his feet shouting, "Bravo! Bravo!" At the same time the huge crowd arose as one body with thunderous applause and various vocal expressions.

I was laughing with joy and shaking my head in disbelief that the celebration of forgiveness and redemption could be so exhilarating. I was both participant and spectator. The celebration of forgiveness left me highly energized and ready to live for my Redeemer.

Leslie F. Brandt stated that celebration and service are twin sisters.

Celebration energizes us for service. But service is different for each recipient of forgiveness. Some sing. Others write. A few preach. Many live self-sacrificially. All are conduits for forgiveness that leads others to the Forgiver. Celebrating and serving in this world acts as an appetizer for the privilege of celebrating and serving throughout eternity. Practicing is a joy when you anticipate the ultimate in celebrating and serving.

My granddaughter Jamie and her Arabian horse, Emerald, practiced for many months to perfect the formations of dressage. She committed the maneuvers to memory and rode them until they became almost second nature. The big day came when she entered the national youth competition in New Mexico. The judges selected her fifth in the top 10 of her class. Talk about celebration!

If you think celebrating forgiveness and serving your forgiving God is a joy now, wait until you celebrate and serve in eternity!

We are not the only ones celebrating forgiveness and forgivingness. God and all the heavenly hosts celebrate whenever the streams of forgiveness flow to and through a repentant sinner. We see this colorfully emphasized in the three lost-and-found stories of Luke 15.

After the shepherd found his sheep afflicted with wanderlust, he carried it on his shoulders, shouting his joy as he made his way home. There he called all his family, friends, and neighbors to celebrate. Jesus commented that great joy fills heaven when just one sinner is redeemed.

One author has suggested that the sheep may not have been a soft woolly lamb or ewe, but a stubborn, obstreperous buck that was not the easiest animal to handle. It's an interesting thought that cannot be proved, but it does say that God is interested in finding all of His lost people, even those who may present problems. It encourages me because I have been difficult for God to handle at times, but He never gives up on me. He's ready to put me on His shoulders and restore me to His fold.

The woman relentlessly searched the house for the coin that

had rolled into the dust and darkness. She no doubt gave a shout heard by the neighbors when she found it. Oh, it was dirty, but she knew it was still silver. She called her neighbors for a big party to celebrate. Jesus commented that the angels are jubilant whenever a sinner is saved.

If you ever feel soiled and unfit, it is important to remember that God goes to great bother to find you. It doesn't matter how you feel about yourself. God knows how to make you sparkle like new. He longs to celebrate your renewal.

The prodigal father found his headstrong son in a terrible condition. Because I used to clean the pigpen on the farm before my father felt convicted to quit raising swine I can easily imagine how that boy must have smelled. That did not deter the father. He threw his mantle around the boy's shoulders, slipped the family ring on his hand, and handed him a pair of new sandals so the boy could walk comfortably. That sandal gift is an important part of the story for me.

Hobos often stopped at our farm for food and a place to sleep. I always noticed their feet. Some of their shoes were so worn that they tied cardboard to the bottoms of them. A few of them had shoes too large for their feet. My father convinced one of them to stay and work on the farm. The first thing he bought him was a sturdy pair of shoes. The prodigal father's son needed new shoes to walk home. He had to look respectable when he crossed the threshold. That says a lot about how interested God is in every aspect of our restoration.

When they arrived home, the father said, "We have to be merry and rejoice because the dead has come to life, the lost has been found." He threw a big party in honor of his returned son.

When I read about thousands of people being baptized into the body of Christ, all I can think is that heaven must be ringing with joyful singing every day. All heaven must be celebrating forgiveness.

The prophet John had visions of Jesus' victory over evil. He heard singing in heaven. In Revelation 4 and 5 he tells about heavenly beings proclaiming praise to the Creator and Redeemer. Especially they sing about Jesus dying to purchase a people for God from every part of the globe. The music must surpass any that I have ever heard. Imagine all the hosts of heaven singing the great "Hallelujah Chorus!"

I was just 14 when I listened to my brother-in-law's record player pumping out the strains of Heartwounds and Samuel Barber's "Adagio for Strings." He sang along with the orchestra. His music captivated me. At 16 I left home to attend a boarding school in Philadelphia. My brother-in-law let me take some of his albums. Using a teacher's player, I listened and sang along with them. Sometimes I even pretended I was the conductor.

One rainy Saturday evening I hopped on a trolley car and made my way to the concert hall of the Philadelphia Symphony Orchestra under the baton of the animated Eugene Ormandy. I stood in the rain for almost an hour waiting for the ticket office to open. By the time I climbed to my seat in the next-to-the highest balcony, my clothes were uncomfortably wet. All my misery vanished, however' when the orchestra opened the program with Barber's "Adagio for Strings." It didn't sound anything like the records. The sensation that I had was that of living on a planet swept with joy. I wanted the music to go on and on.

When I read about the songs of celebration in John's book of Revelation, I long to be swept from earth to heaven so I can hear the oratorio of Redemption, far more moving than the lyrics recorded by the prophet.

Even more astounding is the fact that my forgiveness and forgivingness cause the music of heaven to crescendo and grow in sweetness of melody. I have often wished I knew how to compose thrilling music, but when I open my life to God's forgiving mercy, I enable the heavenly chorus to create music far more majestic than the greatest human masterpiece. All who are born again give birth to newer and sweeter arias, recitatives, and choruses.

When my wife and I ride in the car and listen to classical music stations, sometimes we hear compositions that have no melody. The music is confusing and troubling. We turn it off immediately. The late

Leonard Bernstein once gave a lecture about how modern music was full of despair. He said he labored with young musicians, trying to get them to create sweeter music, but they cannot write music different from what is inside of them.

The music of heaven is truly celebration music, because it has no trace of despair. The joy of our redemption dominates every anthem.

My favorite CD is the Robert Shaw Men's Chorus singing songs of Schubert. I listen to it as I work on my word processor and while I am resting in my recliner. I envy those men. If only I could sing well enough to join them. I sing along with them in the privacy of my home, but I would never pass an audition. Maybe you struggle with the same vocal inadequacy. If so, take heart. We will all sing in heaven before the throne.

We will perform with the Heavenly Harps Orchestra in the Song of the Lamb. Here are the words to the song. Learn them well so you'll be in good form when we perform. "Great and marvelous are Your works, O Lord God, the Almighty; righteous and true are Your ways, King of the nations! Who will not fear, O Lord, and glorify Your name? For You alone are holy; for all the nations will come and worship before You, for Your righteous acts have been revealed" (Rev. 15:3, 4).

That's just one song we will do. I have an idea that John didn't have room to write the words to all of them. Never mind that we don't know all the songs now, just show up for the concert. We will all be in good voice for that celebration.

Recently I attended a Men of Faith conference. During a "song service" we mindlessly sang familiar songs. Some were looking around the auditorium, some were barely mouthing the words, and some were even talking to their friends. John Thurber, the song leader, stopped us. He told us that we were supposed to be praising God and expressing our love and joy about forgiveness and salvation. Look at the words, he told us, feel their importance, and then sing them as we would say them to God. John treated us like a large chorus, stopping us when we sang flatly, and demonstrating how to put our hearts into our song.

In just a few minutes he had transformed a group of listless singers into a chorus of celebration. Before he ended the singing, he invited every man who had ever sung in a quartet or chorus to come to the large platform. There he separated us into basses, baritones, and tenors. Then he announced that we'd sing "Pass Me Not, O Gentle Savior" without music or words in front of us. It was a familiar song. Sing from the bottom of your hearts, he urged us. Oh, how we sang!

When we sing in the celebration of forgiveness we will all have deep gratitude for God and His mercy. We will sing from our experience. There will be no listless mouthing of words. Unlike the one-day Men of Faith singing experience, we will gather every Sabbath before the throne of God and set the universe ringing with our voices. I have a strong notion that we will have the largest repertoire of any chorus that has ever performed.

The celebration of forgiveness will be exciting because all of God's children from every land and every age will be there. The eleventh chapter of Hebrews lists many of the ancient people of faith who endured many trials and maintained their faith by their strong hope of a city whose builder and maker is God. They did not receive that city, but died in faith that they would receive it in the future. God planned for them to await the resurrection at the Second Advent so that we can all go to the celebration together. It will be like a massive reunion. Imagine singing in that throng.

The reason for excitement becomes even more personal for each of us. Every Friday night my mother played the old upright piano while I played my cornet. My father sat in a rocker, tilted his head back, and sang heartily. We'll be there singing together. My son played trumpet, guitar, and sang a few of his own compositions, but a crash in 1980 stilled his voice. He will be there, probably longing to join the angelic brass choir. Our loved ones silenced by death will be silent no longer. Can you imagine missing such a celebration?

Luke 14 records the story of a man who threw a banquet. The people on his original invitation list made a bunch of ridiculous excuses for not coming. The man couldn't see all that food go to waste, and besides, he loved company. It didn't take long to summon his slave. He sent him into the streets and lanes of the city to bring the poor, crippled, blind, and lame to the celebration. The slave took a head count and told his master that they still had plenty of room left. His master sent him into the highways and hedges with the order to compel people to come. The reason? "That my house may be filled" (verse 23).

It isn't difficult for me to believe this story. I've met people like him. In New Haven, Connecticut, a group of Christmas carolers sang in front of all the homes situated on a long ridge overlooking the city. It took the entire evening to complete.

Betsy, one of the carolers, was a nurse in the city hospital. While she was caring for a very ill man he asked her if she attended church. She told him she belonged to the Seventh-day Adventist Church on Humphrey Street. His face brightened with a smile as he said, "Oh, you're the people who sing carols for us every year!"

When Betsy told him she was one of the carolers, he was very grateful, not only for her care, but also for the joy the carolers brought to him at Christmastime. "Betsy, I'm going to invite all the people on my street to my house this Christmas," he told her. "You bring all your carolers to my house to entertain us in the warmth of my home. We'll have food and plenty of time to get acquainted. I'll make a donation to your church for all my guests."

The next Christmas the carolers came prepared to present a beautiful program of Christmas cheer. People crowded the house with its tables laden with fancy food and holiday drinks. It was also filled with laughter and singing and making of new friends.

Our forgiving Lord is not willing for any of His children to miss the celebration of forgiveness. All are invited. He is eager to engage us in spreading the invitation. Jesus paid for our privilege to attend. A banquet will be spread. We will meet people from every land and language group amid laughter and singing. His house will be full.

When I was a member of the Lions Club we hosted a big banquet for those who were blind or visually impaired. The best catering service in town prepared the food. We hired a band to play old favorites and asked a humorist to bring laughter to our guests. Since none of the guests could see well enough to drive, the members of the club drove to their homes and brought them to the banquet and took them home afterward.

The man in the banquet story of Luke 14 provided the same courtesy. He had the guests brought to the party. Jesus and the angel hosts will bring us to the celebration of forgiveness. The escort party will arrive with trumpet blast and mighty shouts from Jesus and the archangel. The graves of the faithful will have no power to hold their inhabitants. God's people will be assembled and transported to the heavenly banquet hall.

The heavenly hosts will escort us to the celebration, but not because we are blind. The Scripture says that when Jesus comes we will be changed in the blink of an eye. The tongue of the mute will sing, the eyes of the blind will be open, the deaf will hear, and the lame will leap like a deer. God will take us to the celebration because we are His. All heaven has waited for this moment, and our arrival will be with fanfare.

A Bible teacher at Washington Missionary College (now Washington Adventist University) retired long after the usual retirement age. Instead of moving to the popular areas where many retired ministers settled, he announced that he would live in a little-known town in Texas. "But why there?" his colleagues asked. "I have an appointment with a little curly-haired girl," he explained. "She is my daughter and sleeping in Jesus. I want to live there so that when Jesus comes I can meet her. My wife and I want to join her on the trip to heaven."

The teacher was apparently looking forward to the trip, not just the privilege of attending the celebration. The apostle Paul said that we will all be caught up together in the air and then transported to our heavenly home.

When our sons were young they constantly plagued us with the question "When are we going to get there?" I seriously doubt that we will be interested in asking that question on the way to heaven. Our trip to the celebration will be so filled by reunions with loved ones that we will not be aware of the passage of time.

When I taught school my pupils loved to imagine what heaven will be like, but they also used lots of imagination about what the trip there would be like. An education supervisor visited my classroom when we were having Bible class. The students were talking about what they thought going to heaven and living there will be like. Some of their concepts were very fanciful, but to them they were possible. At the end of the class the supervisor told me that I had allowed the students to spend too much time imagining what it will be like. She thought I should have used most of the time telling them how to get there and how to get ready for the trip. But I disagreed with her, much to her disapproval. I told her that if the students weren't excited about the trip and the destination, they certainly weren't going to be interested in learning how to get there.

I still allow my imagination to run free. In 1957 a church education leader confirmed the value of this when he told my students about an invalid living in the South. He took his students to visit the man because the individual was excited about heaven and the new earth. One of the students asked the sick man what he did all day. "Oh," the man said, "I am building a house." The children asked how he could put up a house when he couldn't walk. "That's not a problem," the man explained. "You see, right now I am drawing the plans. I won't actually begin construction until I live in the earth made new. Look under my bed. Pull that roll of paper out and open it on the bed. I'll tell you all about the house I'm going to build." The children became excited about his house, and some of them began to dream about their own special house.

What are you going to do on your journey to the celebration of forgiveness? What will the festivities be like? Why not allow your imagination to work overtime?

From the time I was born until I graduated from college my uncle Scotty was the first elder of my hometown church. He almost always had the pastoral prayer during the worship service except when the pastor came every third or fourth week. My uncle prayed from the heart in a voice that was natural and earnest in tone. The ending of his prayer was always the same: "'And, Lord, when You come, we will look up and say, 'Lo, this is our God; we have waited for him, and he will save us: this is the Lord; we have waited for him, we will be glad and rejoice in his salvation!' [Isa. 25:9, KJV]."

In my mind I tried to picture Jesus' second coming. I'd look up at the clouds and imagine that Christ and His angels were breaking through the clouds. But when I thought of myself shouting, "Lo, this is our God!" somehow that expression didn't fit me. I always assumed that I'd be more excited than that. Those words seemed pretty tame to me. Recently I have a different picture in mind. I think many will clap their hands or wave their arms and yell, "Look! It's Jesus!" Some will prostrate themselves on the ground in reverence for the forgiving Savior. Perhaps I am more likely to look up speechless with tears streaming down my face. I imagine many will softly repeat, "Thank You, Jesus. Hallelujah. Praise be to God." My uncle Scotty will no doubt say what he did for so many years—"Lo, this is our God; we have waited for him, and he will save us."

It doesn't matter what we say when we see Jesus. He will be coming to take us to the banquet, the celebration of forgiveness. The trip and the celebration will far surpass anything we have ever dreamed. Won't you come? We can enjoy the celebration together.

We invite you to view the complete
selection of titles we publish at:

www.TEACHServices.com

Please write or e-mail us your praises, reactions, or
thoughts about this or any other book we publish at:

TEACH Services, Inc.
P U B L I S H I N G
www.TEACHServices.com ● (800) 367-1844

P.O. Box 954
Ringgold, GA 30736

info@TEACHServices.com

TEACH Services, Inc., titles may be purchased in bulk for
educational, business, fund-raising, or sales promotional use.
For information, please e-mail:

BulkSales@TEACHServices.com

Finally, if you are interested in seeing
your own book in print, please contact us at

publishing@TEACHServices.com

We would be happy to review your manuscript for free.

www.ingramcontent.com/pod-product-compliance
Lightning Source LLC
Chambersburg PA
CBHW060544100426
42742CB00013B/2441